Praise for *Your Un*

"Bishop Owensby is one of the finest thinkers and writers on today's scene, religious or secular. I read everything he publishes, and I learn something, think deeply, and am moved every time I do. This book is no different. You'll learn, think, be moved, and live a bit differently."
—The Most Rev. Michael B. Curry, 27th Presiding Bishop and Primate of The Episcopal Church

"Drawing on his tremendous gift as a storyteller, Owensby uses his experiences as a guide to connect us to the deep truths that are held in our own stories. We are invited to look at the truths about ourselves that are revealed in our stories of struggle and brokenness, as well as in our stories of joy. From that holy place, we can begin to see with new eyes the places in our lives where God's forgiveness and love have been present. Connecting our stories to God's story, we are invited to grow in our understanding of what it means to be God's beloved."
—The Rt. Rev. Laura J. Ahrens, Bishop Suffragan of The Episcopal Church in Connecticut

"With unmatched charm and disarming clarity, Bishop Jake Owensby invites us to be vulnerable to ourselves, to one another, and to our God. Be warned: your life will never be the same after encountering Jesus in the stories told by Jake."
—The Rt. Rev. Todd Ousley, Bishop for the Office of Pastoral Development

"'We are all in the middle of our story . . . and what has happened to us is still unfolding.' So begins this noteworthy narrative that unlocks memories, explores faith as one who has been 'in the trenches,' and consistently points to the way of Jesus as a guide for the reader toward the extraordinary love that God has for each human being on this planet. The consistent invitation to think about and tell one's own story in light of each chapter's theme is a particular strength and lends itself to strong discussion material for book groups. I recommend this book to you if you have a life story with which you struggle or one in which you wonder where God went. You will find a kind, compassionate, and humble pastor in Bishop Owensby—one who has 'been there' and will help you discover a transforming path for yourself."

—The Rev. Carole Wageman, author of *The Light Shines Through: Our Stories Are God's Story*, www.carolewageman.com

"*Your Untold Story* is an invitation to sift through the libraries of our own spiritual narratives and see the hand of God at work in us— plying us, shaping us, loving us—into becoming our own manifestations of the Body of Christ. Bishop Owensby's book affirms that each of us is called us to reconciliation and restoration. One path to this wholeness is to connect our stories with the eternal, healing story of God. It is a path well worth taking."

—The Rt. Rev. Dr. Audrey Scanlan, Episcopal Diocese of Central Pennsylvania

"Bishop Jake Owensby is a consummate storyteller. In *Your Untold Story* he recounts wonderful stories and arresting encounters in his own experience and then, in sometimes quite surprising ways, ties them to stories in the Scriptures. In so doing he not only deepens our appreciation of the biblical narratives that shape us, but he invites us to be tellers of our own stories, especially those still untold that need to be shared. An inspiring and fun read!"

—The Rt. Rev. J. Neil Alexander, Vice President and Dean of the School of Theology at University of the South, Sewanee, Tennessee

Your Untold Story

Tales of a Child of God

Jake Owensby

Church Publishing
NEW YORK

Unless otherwise noted, the scripture quotations contained herein are from the New Revised Standard Version Bible, copyright © 1989 by the Division of Christian Education of the National Council of Churches of Christ in the U.S.A. Used by permission. All rights reserved.

Church Publishing
19 East 34th Street
New York, NY 10016
www.churchpublishing.org

Cover design by Jennifer Kopec, 2Pug Design
Typeset by PerfecType

Library of Congress Cataloging-in-Publication Data
Names: Owensby, Jacob, 1957- author.
Title: Your untold story : tales of a child of God / Jake Owensby.
Description: New York : Church Publishing, 2018. | Includes index.
Identifiers: LCCN 2017035468 (print) | LCCN 2017047970 (ebook) | ISBN
   9781640650053 (ebook) | ISBN 9781640650046 (pbk.)
Subjects: LCSH: Identity (Psychology)--Religious aspects--Christianity. |
   Storytelling--Religious aspects--Christianity. | Jesus Christ--Example. |
   Witness bearing (Christianity)
Classification: LCC BV4509.5 (ebook) | LCC BV4509.5 .O935 2018 (print) | DDC
   248.4/83--dc23
LC record available at https://lccn.loc.gov/2017035468

Printed in the United States of America

To Patrick, Meredith, and Andrew

CONTENTS

Acknowledgments xi

Introduction xv

Part One: Reimagining Jesus

All They're Going to Get Is You 3

Keeping Our Word 7

In Our Very Bones 11

Jesus and Nietzsche Walk into a Bar 15

Jesus, Clark Kent, and Quentin Tarantino 19

Part Two: Retelling Your Story

Hearing Grace 25

Forgiving Yourself 29

Boiled Shrimp and Broken Toys 33

Restoring Our Sanity 37

Stretching Each Other 41

Part Three: Family, Friends, and Other Strangers

Being Normal Almost Killed Me 47

Ugly Love 51

Not Those People 55

Walls and Bridges 59

Claudia, Her Sisters, and the Ascension 63

Lies and Secrets and Funerals 67

Part Four: The Sense of an Ending

Even This 73

A Happier Place 77

Dirty Laundry 81

Until Morning 85

Appendix A: Scripture Index 89

Appendix B: Scripture Stories 91

My story is important not because it is mine, God knows, but because if I tell it anything like right, the chances are you will recognize that in many ways it is also yours. . . . It is precisely through these stories in all their particularity, as I have long believed and often said, that God makes himself known to each of us more powerfully and personally. If this is true, it means that to lose track of our stories is to be profoundly impoverished not only humanly but also spiritually.

—Frederick Buechner, *Telling Stories*

Tell all the truth but tell it slant.

—Emily Dickinson

ACKNOWLEDGMENTS

Writing is a spiritual practice for me. Each morning I spend time thinking and praying at my keyboard. While this may sound like a solitary pursuit, it is nothing of the kind. I bring a web of interconnected communities with me into my study. This book has grown out of my relationship with those communities, so I want to extend my gratitude to them.

On most Sundays I travel to one of the congregations in the Episcopal Diocese of Western Louisiana. Some of these faith communities are large and reside in cities. Most are small. Humble main streets and lush farmland form their setting. People have shared their lives and hopes and concerns with me on my visitations. Their hopes and concerns shape my reading and writing, and I am deeply grateful to these people for letting me into their lives.

The readership of my blog includes people in my diocese and extends far beyond its borders. "Looking for God in Messy Places"[1] has become for me a sort of community. At the blog, on social media, and in private e-mails, readers respond to my thoughts with their own stories, with their intellectual objections, and, frankly, sometimes with their contempt. I am deeply grateful for all of this. These interactions continue to enlarge my perspective and shape my reflections.

My colleagues in the House of Bishops have been and continue to be a rich source of inspiration and encouragement. When we gather we bring the demographic and theological diversity of our respective dioceses along with us. Frequently I come away from our meetings with an expanded understanding of the challenges we face and the myriad ways in which grace weaves itself into our lives. This book has been shaped by these insights. I am deeply grateful to my colleagues

---

1. You can find it at https://jakeowensby.com.

and especially grateful to those who have shared words and notes of encouragement about my writing.

The clergy of my diocese have formed a close, supportive, and inclusive community. They face sometimes daunting ministry challenges with grace and fearless creativity. At our gatherings their theological exchanges and spiritual reflections have set my mind and heart spinning in ways that inevitably show up in my writing. Their responses to and support of my writing ministry have sustained me and encouraged me.

My spiritual director Dennis Campbell helped me to clarify who I am as a writer. In our discussions I came to realize that I am a bishop who writes, not a writer who happens to be a bishop. Thanks to our work together, I understand this book as an example of my service to a network of communities.

Whatever virtues my writing embodies owes much to my wonderful editor, Sharon Ely Pearson. Having the support of a friend with such talent, energy, and grace is simply a gift. I am deeply grateful for her guidance and encouragement. Sharon's colleagues—Ryan Masteller at Church Publishing and Amy Wagner—shaped my manuscript into the well-crafted book it is now. I admire their remarkable gifts and appreciate the time, energy, and care they spent on this project.

The excellence, dedication, and faithfulness of my staff make it possible for me to devote the time I do to writing. Kathy Richey, Holly Davis, Joy Owensby, Ron Clingenpeel, Bill Bryant, Bette Kaufmann, Bob Harwell, and Liz Ratcliffe are committed to the missional vision of this diocese and to serving God's people here. I trust them, admire them, and give thanks for them. I would also like to acknowledge the keen eye of Sonny Carter, whose photo of me you'll find on the back cover of this book.

As you may have noted, this book is dedicated to my sons and my daughter. Patrick, Andrew, and Meredith are all adults now. Each of them in their way has been a conduit of grace in my life. They have softened me and strengthened me. They have taught me what love is and how much more diverse God's children are than I had once imagined. I am grateful for them and love them to the moon and back.

And I'm also grateful that they still seem to enjoy having fun at their dad's expense.

Finally, I am grateful for and to my wife, Joy. Theological conversations and spiritual reflections frequently lace our morning walks and our late evening talks. Joy listens. She tells me honestly when I'm being opaque and when I'm being a blunt instrument. Her kindness and thoughtfulness and wisdom are starting to rub off on me. At least, I hope they are. If you recognize anything like those traits in the chapters that follow, you can be sure that much of the credit belongs to Joy.

INTRODUCTION

A large holiday cookie tin sat on the hearth in the den of my father's house. My wife, Joy, and I pried the top off while no one was looking. A jumbled heap of old photographs filled three-quarters of the container. My father figured prominently in each picture. Some were in color. Some in black and white. Holding up a shot of him posing on a beach, Joy said, "Jake, I think all these pictures have been cut in half."

A young, trim Sam Owensby in swimming trunks smiled back at the camera. His right arm was draped around a woman at his side. Only, someone had snipped all of her from the scene except for a small portion of her bare shoulder and the strap of her bathing suit. Joy and I began shuffling through the rest of the photos. A few were intact. But most had been trimmed down to half or three-quarters or just a sliver. I was puzzled until I realized that all of these pictures had been taken while my parents were still married. My father had clipped out the images of my mother.

My parents had divorced years earlier. Married at that time to his third wife, my father seemed to want these photos to portray his life as if my mother had never been in it. In that moment, the story I had been telling myself about my father began revising itself. Or more accurately, I realized that I had simply been accepting my father's version of his story. And crucially, I began to see that the narratives I told of myself and of my mother and of my family of origin and of everyone I met had been shaped by my desire to be faithful to my father's account of who he was.

My father was a natural storyteller. As a little boy I sat spellbound while he spun tales of his Depression-era childhood in a South

Carolina mill village. The youngest of thirteen children, he was a notorious prankster and charming rebel—Gaffney's own Huck Finn. At other times he told war stories. At fifteen, he had lied about his age and joined the Navy to serve in the Pacific theater of World War II. Whether manning an antiaircraft gun or piloting a landing craft onto enemy beaches, my father braved enemy bullets and impressed his fellow sailors with his courage and ferocity.

At least, that's how the stories went. My father's stories always featured him as the hero. As I grew older, I noticed that the details changed, but the stories always aimed to achieve the same result: the admiration of Sam Owensby. In an old Southern tradition captured in films like *Big Fish*, my father was a fabulist. Mind you, stretching the truth can be sort of enchanting. But it can have toxic effects.

I always felt the need to remain faithful to my father's story about himself. As pathetic as it may sound, I craved my father's approval. My yearning for his praise and affection was no doubt magnified because they were so obviously conditional. The result was that I struggled to tell a true story about myself to myself. A recurring theme of my unwritten autobiography was that I never measured up. Over time, this and various other toxic themes were killing me. Eventually, I went looking for a new way to tell my story. I found that new way in the stories of Jesus.

Jesus once said, "I am the Truth." There are plenty of ways to read these words. And in this book I hear them encouraging me to tell the true story about myself and about other people by trying to stay faithful to the stories of Jesus. Every story that remains faithful to Jesus' story has one overriding motif: I am a beloved child of God and so is everyone I meet.

Saying that we are beloved children of God and living it— experiencing it viscerally—are two different things. We have to tell and retell our stories—and the stories of other people—as we encounter the stories of Jesus. As we come to know Jesus more intimately, we come to see ourselves with more gracious clarity and others with a more compassionate tenderness. We are never finished with this storytelling. The depth of God's love for us is infinite. Our growth in intimacy with God and one another has an infinite trajectory.

I invite you to join me in telling your untold story. You can do so on your own or in a group. The chapters are organized into four parts. You don't have to follow this order. Every chapter can stand on its own. But you may also find it helpful to follow the sequence I've offered.

Part one focuses on the identity of Jesus. Each chapter provides an opportunity to expand and deepen your understanding of Jesus and to encounter his unrelenting love. The stories in part two invite you to revise the story you tell about yourself in light of your renewed Jesus story. The aim is to help you experience yourself as a beloved child of God. In part three we turn to telling stories about strangers, friends, and family members as beloved children of God like us. Finally, part four reminds us that the story of our life is not yet over. We are all in the middle of our story. The meaning of what we have done and what has happened to us is still unfolding. We anticipate an ending that will show us that meaning, but we have not gotten there yet. Eternal life is the ending we anticipate. So this final section dwells on what we mean by eternal life and how that vision affects our day-to-day lives.

Each chapter engages a passage of scripture and provides that passage for your convenience. Reflection questions conclude each chapter. The goal throughout is to help you tell your untold story and to hear the untold story of your friends and the strangers you meet: the untold tales of a child of God.

Part One

Reimagining Jesus

Jesus did not come to change the mind of God about humanity; Jesus came to change the mind of humanity about God.
—Richard Rohr, "Incarnation Instead of Atonement,"
Daily Meditation, February 12, 2016

I have never said that I am a good Christian. I just know that Jesus adores me and is only as far away as His name. I say, "Hi, Lord," and He says, "Hello, darling." He loves me so much He keeps a photo of me in His wallet.
—Anne Lamott, "Like a Puppy in a Christmas Stocking,"
interview with *World Magazine*, September 20, 2003

Chapter 1

All They're Going to Get Is You

Read Luke 17:5–10.

Don Armentrout stood tall enough to ride the big rollercoasters at Six Flags. His balding head formed a kind of natural tonsure, and he peered through eyewear that resembled twin magnifying glasses. When I was a seminarian at the School of Theology in Sewanee, Tennessee, Don delivered his Church History lectures at a torrid clip, frequently hiking his sagging khakis back up to his waist as he said, "You know what I mean?" We all struggled to keep pace with him in our notes and breathed a sigh of relief whenever he started in on one of his brief asides. One day, he said something like this: "When you get out there in your churches, people are going to come looking for Jesus. And all they're going to get is you. You better think about that."

I'm still thinking about that. And now I'm asking you to think about that. All sorts of people are looking for God. God took up flesh and moved into the neighborhood. God comes to meet us in Jesus. And here's the catch: since the Ascension and the descent of the Spirit, we are the only Body that Jesus has. People will come looking for Jesus, and they're only going to get us. And that's exactly how God designed it. To borrow from Sting's song "Every Breath We Take," every move we make, every breath we take represents Jesus to the world. God expects us to represent Jesus in the way he deserves. God's mission of reconciliation and restoration hinges on it.

All sorts of people felt welcome around Jesus. The handicapped, the contagious, and foreigners approached him without hesitation. His regular dinner companions included notorious crooks and women of ill repute. Jesus brought healing and sanity. He fed the hungry and forgave the people who wounded him. If you were down and out, flat on your back, or on everybody's scumbag list, Jesus was on your side.

People are looking for Jesus today. And all they're going to get is us.

Jesus as much as told his disciples the same thing. For instance, after wrestling with the condescending, judgmental religious leaders of his day, he took the disciples aside and gave them a mini-lesson in how to look like Jesus.[1] To paraphrase he said, "Don't be a stumbling block to anybody else. Your thoughts, words, and deeds have a ripple effect. Whether you realize it or not, you can knock somebody else out of the boat. Hurt people hurt people. Jerks make jerks. You'd be better off having an anchor tied around your neck and being thrown into the bayou. Heal and nurture instead. Oh, and while you're at it, forgive. And keep forgiving. If the same boneheads have to apologize seven times a day every single day, forgive them. Sure, you'll start to think that their remorse is insincere. God will sort that out. Forgive them."

Squirming at what they were hearing, they said, "Increase our faith!" We're doing the same, I suspect. These expectations are too high. Nobody can live up to them. So give us the faith to accomplish what you ask!

You might think that Jesus would break out the gold stars for this response. But instead of a hearty pat on the back, Jesus gives them a verbal smack on the back of the head. He tells the disciples—and he's telling us—that we've completely missed the boat about faith. Faith is not something we have that makes us capable of remarkable things. Having a stronger faith has nothing to do with holding more tenaciously to our ideas about God.

---

1. Luke 17:1–10.

Faith is a relationship. Jesus initiates and sustains that relationship by being faithful to us. He sticks by us and gives himself to us. Our faith is a response. It happens—and its contours change—one day at a time, and those days have a cumulative effect.

The various saints on our liturgical calendar show us that a faithful life amounts to a Jesus-saturated life. A faithful life is one in which Jesus does uncanny, unexpected, holy things. Saints don't accomplish things so much as Jesus makes things happen in and through them. Saints show us what it means to be the Body of Christ.

Plenty of saints never make it onto the Church's calendar. History will not record most of their names. But we recognize them when we see them. They are representing Jesus in a way that makes us say, "Oh! Right! That's it!"

For instance, about ten years ago we saw Jesus in the Amish community. Charlie Roberts walked into a one-room schoolhouse near Lancaster, Pennsylvania, and opened fire. He killed five children and wounded five others. Then he took his own life.

Charlie's mother, Terri, will never forget that day. Her husband said, "I will never face my Amish neighbors again."[2] A few days later, the Robertses buried their son in a small, private ceremony. As they came to the gravesite, they saw forty members of the Amish community approaching. The Amish enfolded the Roberts family in a semicircle, extending forgiveness and sharing grief. In their sorrow, shame, and loneliness, the Robertses came looking for Jesus that day, whether they knew it or not. All they got was the Amish. And on that day, a small, wounded group of Amish were the real Jesus.

That's who we want to be for the addict and the parolee, for the lonely teenager and the disabled vet, for the cynical banker and the calloused farmer, for the streetwalker and the street cleaner. We want

---

2. "A Decade after Amish School Shooting, Gunman's Mother Talks of Forgiveness," *NPR Morning Edition*, September 30, 2016, http://www.npr.org/2016/09/30/495905609/a-decade-after-amish-school-shooting-gunman-s-mother-talks-of-forgiveness?utm_campaign=storyshare&utm_source=facebook.com&utm_medium=social.

to bring healing and compassion and peace to overscheduled families and exhausted night-shift workers. To blue lives and black lives. To bow-tied professionals and professional slackers. We want to be Jesus to whomever we meet.

It saddens me when what some Christians say or do misrepresent Jesus as condescending and exclusionary. For instance, famous preachers have condemned Muslims for being, well, Muslim. Christian business owners have insisted on the right to refuse service to same-sex couples as an expression of religious freedom. Their words and actions portray Jesus as focused solely on a single moral or political agenda. As quarrelsome and scornful. As resentful and morally smug. We know, or at least we are supposed to know, that Jesus came not to condemn but to save. And yet all too often we forget how to embody the inclusive graciousness that is the sacred heart of Jesus.

God realizes that these infinite standards are too high for us injured, timid, fractious humans to meet. That's why God became one of us and lived in our midst and dwells in our hearts. We are not in this alone. We are the Body of Christ. People are looking for Jesus. And all they're going to get is us. Let's keep thinking about that.

Reflection Questions

1. What word, phrase, image, or idea in this chapter stood out to you? What ideas, stories, images, or questions did it suggest to you?

2. Does this chapter confirm, challenge, or enlarge your image of Jesus? Talk about how this is so for you.

3. Have you ever experienced a moment when you said, "Oh! Right! That's it!" Talk about a time when you learned something new about Jesus or came to know Jesus at a greater depth in the actions, words, or attitudes of another person.

4. Can you recall or imagine a time that someone else might have encountered Jesus in you? What do you think they learned about him?

Chapter 2

Keeping Our Word

Read John 14:23–29.

When our oldest son, Andrew, was about three, he loved climbing things. Ladders, trellises, trees—they all beckoned him to clamber up toward the roof or the sky. In the house, we found Andrew mounting our coffee table and leaping off. Not wanting him to mar the furniture or bump his head, we told him not to do that. Since this made no sense to him, he kept scaling the coffee table and leaping off, only to have us put him in time-out for a count of ten. Eventually, he got the point. At least, he got *a* point.

When he thought I wasn't looking, Andrew got on the table and jumped off. Before I could say anything, and without having seen me, he said, "Time-out!" He walked to the accustomed corner, counted to ten, returned to the table, and repeated the process a few more times. That wasn't quite what we had had in mind.

Sometimes I suspect that Jesus looks at his Church and, with patience and love, shakes his head and thinks, "That wasn't quite what I had in mind." Jesus had said, "Those who love me will keep my word."[1] With all the best intentions, people have taken his words to heart. And gotten them completely wrong. They assume that Jesus means, "If you love me, you will follow the rules I've given you." Sincerely trying

---

1. John 14:23.

7

to follow Jesus, some people believe that Jesus' word—his *logos*—is a moral code. A set of dos and don'ts.

But let's do a quick review of Jesus' teaching in John's Gospel. Again and again he says, "I am." You know, like God speaking to Moses in the burning bush. "I AM WHO I AM."[2] Jesus identifies himself as God incarnate. As God incarnate, he is Living Water, Bread of Life, Light of the World, and Good Shepherd. In other words, the subject matter of Jesus' teaching is Jesus' identity. And Jesus' identity is Love Incarnate.

Jesus teaches us who he is, so that we will know who we are. We are not just Jesus' followers. We are Jesus' Body. Like, really. Our hands and feet and faces are the very Body of Christ. Keeping Jesus' word means to remember who we are. And that is what Jesus is trying to get across in his very last teaching session.

Commentators frequently call chapters 14 through 16 of John's Gospel "The Farewell Discourse." After the Last Supper, Jesus gives his followers an extended teaching. Strictly speaking, Jesus is not saying good-bye for three chapters. Instead, he is preparing his followers to be the postresurrection people of God. To use Presiding Bishop Michael Curry's way of talking, he is inaugurating a new era in the Jesus movement.

To be sure, Jesus does prepare his followers for the crucifixion and for the ascension. Jesus tells them plainly that he is going away on numerous occasions. But they don't get it. The physical presence around which God has gathered the Jesus movement will be absent. Even though Jesus will rise with a spiritual body, he will ascend to his Father's house.

For those accustomed to seeing Jesus' face and hearing his voice and even smelling that Jesus-y fragrance in his hair and his clothes, Jesus will be gone. And even for those to whom the risen Jesus chooses to show himself, the risen body of Jesus will no longer be present. The Jesus they have known will be absent.

He is quick to say, "Don't be discouraged. Don't be afraid." Knowing Jesus as we do, we shouldn't imagine that Jesus tells them

---

2. Exodus 3:14.

to toughen up and to stuff their very human responses into the cellar of their hearts. Instead, Jesus is telling them that he will be present in a new and even more powerful way. His presence among his friends was changing, not ending. And the way in which Jesus was going to be present with his friends *changes them*. Jesus will change them from being his followers into being his Body. The Body of Christ. Jesus is physically present to this world through our hands and our feet.

Our hands and feet are not *metaphorically* the Body of Christ just because we adhere to a set of principles or we're really nice people or we try to do lots of good works. We are the Body of Christ because the Holy Spirit dwells in each of us, guides each of us, spiritually molds us, and, crucially, weaves us together into one. As Paul put it, the same Spirit dwells in each of us.[3] That's why we are many members of one body.

At Baptism, the Holy Spirit comes to dwell in each of us and to weave us into the Body of all the baptized. In the Holy Eucharist we participate ever more fully in the life of the risen Christ. We become what we eat and drink. The Body of Christ.

The spiritual challenge for us is to be who we truly are: to be the Body of Christ. And there is much at stake here. Although not what you may have in mind. Too many of the people of God have fixated on doing what we need to do to get into heaven and how to avoid going to hell. We've made loving Jesus all about getting our own ticket to paradise.

Think about keeping Jesus' word from a different perspective. What we know about anybody in this world comes through our senses. Yes, we intuit and use our heart and our imagination, but we know each other through our eyes and ears. And the world will know Christ through his Body—through you and me. The world will believe in Jesus to the extent that we are believable as the Body of Jesus. And we do not have the luxury of assigning one segment of our lives to doing Christ-like things while reserving the rest of it for all that worldly stuff we really like.

---

3. Romans 8:9, 11; 1 Corinthians 3:16.

Jesus has marked us as his own forever. Every fiber of us. Whatever we do, whenever we do it, we do it as the Body of Christ. We are true to ourselves or we betray ourselves. If we devote our lives to pursuing accomplishments and status, then, when we repeat Jesus' words about dying to self, they will ring false. If we resist dispensing with material comforts so that others may eat and be properly clothed, it should not surprise us when people shrug indifferently at our call to love our neighbor as ourselves. When we seek to protect ourselves from harm by threatening violence against others, we should expect the world to respond with cynicism when we preach a peace not of this world.

Keeping Jesus' word means fleshing out the divine love already present within us in the Holy Spirit. Jesus put it this way: there is no greater love than laying down our life for a friend.[4] And here is our challenge: any friend of Jesus' is a friend of ours. And Jesus chooses everybody as his friend. Simply everybody.

Reflection Questions

1. What word, phrase, image, or idea in this chapter stood out to you? What ideas, stories, images, or questions did it suggest to you?
2. Does this chapter confirm, challenge, or enlarge your image of Jesus? Talk about how this is so for you.
3. This chapter says that the world will believe in Jesus to the extent that we are believable as the Body of Jesus. Can you remember a time that someone else was believable to you as the Body of Jesus?
4. Can you remember or imagine a time that your actions or attitudes made Jesus believable to someone else?

---

4. John 15:13.

Chapter 3

In Our Very Bones

Read Matthew 3:13–17.

If you're traveling north on US 165 from Lake Charles to Alexandria, Louisiana, you'll see the billboard on your left in Oakdale. A man engulfed in flames is turning his anguished face toward a heaven so distant that neither he nor we can see it. The sign reads: "People on earth hate to hear the word 'repent'! People in hell wish they could hear it one more time."

As I recall, the sign mentions neither a congregation nor a denomination. Whoever paid for the billboard seems to have thought that they were conveying the agreed-upon essence of the Christian message. Sadly, plenty of Christians and non-Christians equate the gospel with hell-avoidance. The hell-avoidance version of the gospel goes like this: Stop sinning. Believe that Jesus took the punishment for your sins. Go to heaven. Or, the alternative is to keep sinning. Reject or even ignore Jesus. Go to hell. Well, strictly speaking, even if you're a do-gooder like Gandhi or Anne Frank, you still go to hell if you don't accept Jesus before you die.

Well, this has always seemed a bit off to me.

I remember a conversation in my freshman religion class at St. Pius X Catholic High School in Atlanta. Our teacher—a nun whose name I've regrettably forgotten—asked us if we believed in hell. Could we reconcile the existence of hell with what we had been learning about the doctrine of God and God's infinite grace? Calmly and logically I suggested that since the all-loving God seeks connection with everyone, and that God is omnipotent, God will win over every heart eventually.

Like any Episcopalian, reason plays a crucial role in my faith. My fourteen-year-old mind still needed a lot of theological reading and lacked the rigorous logical training I would eventually receive. But I'm convinced that I was on to something. The beating heart of our faith is the transforming power of God's love. Fear of hell is at best a distraction, at worst a spiritual manipulation.

The perfect revelation of God's love is Jesus. In the pages of scripture, Jesus makes God's mission clear. He is bringing the Kingdom of Heaven to earth. Look, for instance, at Matthew's account of Jesus receiving John's baptism of repentance.[1]

When Jesus emerges from the waters of the Jordan, the heavens open to him. A voice says, "This is my Son, the Beloved." In Mark's account, the voice is speaking to Jesus. According to Matthew, however, we're all getting that divine message. In Jesus, the heavens bend low not merely to touch the earth, but to saturate it. At the very beginning of his ministry, Jesus is already answering the prayer that he will eventually teach his disciples: "Thy kingdom come . . . on earth as it is in heaven." Jesus is more than a gifted teacher and a bold prophet. Jesus is God incarnate. Fully human and fully divine. In the Incarnation God infuses the earthly with the heavenly.

Let me be clear. God is still God. We are still frail, finite creatures. This is not pantheism.[2] But in Jesus we participate in the divine life. We are who we most truly are in our relationship with God. In Jesus, we become the children of God. The fully realized image of God. Eventually.

We can think about how near and essential God is to us on analogy with how important water is to us. Water comprises up to 60

---

1. Matthew 3:13–17.

2. Pantheists believe that God is not distinct from the universe. Or, to put that differently, pantheism is the belief that everything is God.

percent of our bodies as a whole. The percentage is even higher in our brains and our lungs, 73 percent and 83 percent respectively. So, water resides in the depths of our tissues, our blood, and our bones. Water is not a separate limb or organ in our body. No one would point to another person and call her a body of water. But without water we simply wouldn't exist. We would collapse into lifeless dust.

That's one of the lessons conveyed by the waters of Baptism. God seeks to be so closely entwined with our lives that we're God-saturated. Some have explained Baptism as a bath that washes away our sins. But I invite you to think of placing a dry sponge under running water at your sink. The hard, rough block in your hand readily absorbs the water. It increases in size and becomes soft and malleable. Crucially, the sponge grows in its ability to clean things as it becomes saturated. A hard, dry sponge doesn't clean pots and pans or wipe counters very effectively.

From the beginning, God made us for this kind of intimacy with our Maker. In Jesus, God enters our lives and transforms us. We become who and what we were always meant to be. So as it turns out, Jesus is about repentance. What Jesus (and John the Baptist) proclaims bears no resemblance to that ghastly sign along US 165. To repent is to be transformed in your mind, your soul, and your heart by the abiding presence of Christ.

Christ stretches us to overcome prejudices handed down to us in our childhood, to forgive those who injure us, and to respond to the needs of strangers who give us the creeps. We strain to recognize the dignity of every human being, even when those human beings refuse to respect the divinely given dignity in us or in themselves. When someone seeks to utterly undo us, our urge to obliterate the threat collides with Christ's command to love our enemies.

Neither billboards, nor television spots, nor memes that go viral on social media can adequately convey the message of God's transforming love. Only frail, imperfect hands and bruised, fragile hearts can do it. In other words, it's up to you and me. But we are not on our own. The Kingdom has come near. It courses through our veins and resides in our very bones.

Reflection Questions

1. What word, phrase, image, or idea in this chapter stood out to you? What ideas, stories, images, or questions did it suggest to you?
2. Does this chapter confirm, challenge, or enlarge your image of Jesus? Talk about how this is so for you.
3. This chapter talks about living a God-saturated life. Have you known someone whose life seemed to be saturated by God? Have you had experiences of deep intimacy with God? Share a story.
4. In this chapter the author discusses repentance as a change of heart or a change of mind. Have you ever experienced a change about how you see your life or other people? Are you experiencing a change like that now?

Chapter 4

Jesus and Nietzsche Walk into a Bar

Read Luke 21:5–19.

We all hated wind sprints. Fifty yards up and back. Then forty, then thirty, then twenty, and finally ten. My football coach ended most every practice with this particular form of torture. Already exhausted by two hours of running through new plays, working on technique, and full-speed scrimmaging, I dreaded standing in line waiting for the whistle to send each group of five or ten racing down the field. Being the fastest guy on the team has its advantages. It proved a serious negative during sprints. If I didn't win every time, coach knew I was dogging it.

One day my friend Rob gave me his secret to enduring sprints. He said, "I just tell myself that it lasts about ten minutes. They don't last forever. You just have to get through ten minutes." I adopted his approach and it helped. A little. And his words shaped how I thought about endurance for years. Get through it. Dig deep and gut it out. You can do this. You'll be stronger on the other side of a struggle.

From time to time I hear that philosophy summarized in the phrase, "What doesn't kill you makes you stronger." It's a catchy line in a Jack Reacher, tough guy sort of way. And rehearsing that mantra probably adds some motivation in the middle of a CrossFit workout or during marathon training. But as a philosophy of life—especially a Christian philosophy of life—this motto has some problems.

For starters, consider what the author may have meant. Friedrich Nietzsche coined the phrase in his work *Twilight of the Idols.* In that work, Nietzsche advocates a transvaluation or inversion of values. In particular, he criticizes Christianity for inverting nature and being hostile to life. To be fair, Nietzsche says positive things about Jesus in different contexts. But he still ties life's meaning to drawing on our own inner reserves to overcome not only our obstacles but the more limited versions of ourselves. Nietzsche would not advocate central Christian teachings like drawing on a power greater than ourselves and relying upon the transforming power of God's grace.

If these considerations don't persuade you that this is not the slogan for you, then think about one undeniable truth. The death rate remains 100 percent. Self-overcoming stops at the grave. We all die. Drawing solely on our own inner reserves will get us only so far. The final enemy is death. The dead can't pull themselves up by their own bootstraps. In the final analysis, we are all either losers or we must reach beyond ourselves to a power greater than ourselves. Only Jesus raises the dead to new life.

So, when Jesus tells us that those who endure will win their souls, he cannot possibly mean that we should do whatever it takes to preserve our lives. On the contrary, he has said the exact opposite. "For those who want to save their life will lose it, and those who lose their life for my sake will save it."[1] And again, "Those who try to make their life secure will lose it, but those who lose their life will keep it."[2] When he teaches us to endure, Jesus means something more like this: Give God time to heal you. To make you a new creation. The way of Jesus is the way of dying and rising.

Merely getting through horrible experiences alive can leave us dismantled and tormented. As both the son and the father of men who endured combat, I find myself thinking frequently about the

---

1. Luke 9:24.
2. Luke 17:33.

women and men returning from the wars we've been waging for over a decade now. Between 11 and 20 percent of the veterans returning from Operation Iraqi Freedom and Operation Enduring Freedom have suffered from post-traumatic stress disorder. While some recover, an agonizing number of vets live on the streets. More than twenty commit suicide every day.[3]

Less commonly known is the condition called Moral Injury. Thomas Gibbons-Neff, a Marine veteran of Afghanistan, describes the condition this way. In combat, people develop a second self that is capable of killing a perceived threat without hesitation. In Iraq and Afghanistan, women, children, and the elderly will sometimes carry a Kalashnikov or strap on a suicide bomb.[4] This second self contrasts sharply with the first self who visits grandparents on holidays, delivers Thanksgiving meals to the poor, and tucks children into bed with nursery rhymes.

Returning to civilian life, the second self must merge back into the first self. In Moral Injury, sufferers find this nearly impossible to do. A large part of them longs to be back on the battlefield, the place where they feel normal. They can still be excited by the prospect of opening fire when someone cuts them off in traffic. At the same time, they feel how abnormal this is.

Iraq and Afghanistan didn't kill them. But war left them morally adrift and incapable of reconnecting with the community they fought to protect. Men and women suffering from Moral Injury are not weak. But they are shattered, and they lack the resources within themselves to put the pieces back together. Over time, treatment heals the wounds to their moral foundations. The old life dies so that they can receive a new life.

---

3. Leo Shane and Patricia Kane, "New VA Study Finds 20 Veterans Commit Suicide Each Day," *Military Times*, July 7, 2016, http://www.militarytimes.com /story/veterans/2016/07/07/va-suicide-20-daily-research/86788332/.
4. Thomas Gibbons-Neff, "Why Distinguishing a Moral Injury from PTSD Is Important," *Stars and Stripes*, March 9, 2015, http://www.stripes.com/opinion /why-distinguishing-a-moral-injury-from-ptsd-is-important-1.333520.

Those suffering from Moral Injury illustrate for us the Way of Jesus. The way of dying and rising. Jesus does not teach us that God rewards the strong. The winners. The ones who muscle obstacles aside. God restores the shattered. Mends the broken. Returns the lost. Revives the weak.

To endure is to wait. To trust. As Anne Lamott has posted on Facebook and in her Twitter feed,[5] to understand that grace always bats last. Many things will wound us. One day something will kill us. But Jesus is stronger than death. His love makes us a new creation. All he asks is that we give him time.

Reflection Questions

1. What word, phrase, image, or idea in this chapter stood out to you? What ideas, stories, images, or questions did it suggest to you?
2. Does this chapter confirm, challenge, or enlarge your image of Jesus? Talk about how this is so for you.
3. This chapter distinguishes between drawing on your inner strength to endure trials and suffering and reaching out to a power beyond yourself to be transformed by adversity. Talk about how you understand this distinction. Give examples you've seen in others and share experiences you've had of both approaches to life.
4. Have you experienced spiritual growth as a result of trying circumstances? If so, did you experience Christ's presence as key to that transformation? If not, what do you make of the stories people tell about Jesus bringing them to new life?

---

5. https://www.facebook.com/AnneLamott/posts/894203970709247 and https://twitter.com/annelamottquote/status/665582714880307200?lang=en.

Chapter 5

Jesus, Clark Kent, and Quentin Tarantino

Read Luke 23:33–43.

My earliest boyhood reading came mainly from three sources. Over my father's objections, my mother purchased *Compton's Encyclopedia* on a volume-a-month, pay-as-you-go plan. I devoured each one before the next arrived. Somehow a 1950s vintage Boy Scout manual had found its way into our house. I pored over every page. And, finally, with my allowance I purchased every comic book I could get my hands on. Storing them in an old cardboard box, I read them over and over again.

Out of desperation I would sometimes grab an Archie comic or something like it. But those stories about teenaged boys and girls seemed dumb from my preadolescent perspective. Most of my spare change went for superhero comics. Among my favorites were Batman, Spiderman, and Superman. Bruce Wayne became Batman and Peter Parker became Spiderman when they put on their superhero outfits. The costumes hid their everyday identity.

For years I assumed that Superman followed the same storyline, but the movie director Quentin Tarantino eventually set me straight. Superman disguised himself as Clark Kent. He put on a suit and a pair of glasses that made him look like one of us. In Tarantino's film *Kill Bill: Vol. 2*, the character Bill explains the difference between Superman and the other superheroes to his eventual killer, The Bride, or Beatrix Kiddo. Bill says: "Superman didn't become Superman. Superman was born Superman. When Superman wakes up in the morning, he's Superman. His alter ego is Clark Kent. . . . Clark Kent is how Superman views us."[1]

Fans of more recent Superman comics find fault with Tarantino's portrayal of Clark as meek and mild-mannered. After the 1980s, Clark himself was a stronger, more courageous figure. However, what caught my attention and stirred my theological imagination was this: Clark Kent is how Superman views us. It occurred to me that, by analogy, we could say that Jesus is how God views us.

Every analogy is limited. Jesus was *not* a superhero. God did *not* merely put on a human costume. God really became a human being while remaining fully divine. And Jesus reveals God to us in a way that we can understand. Nevertheless, we can translate what Tarantino says about Superman to serve theological purposes. Jesus is how God views us.

We can see this especially in the Transfiguration and the Crucifixion. Peter, James, and John ascend a mountain with Jesus. Once at the top, Jesus' face and clothing begin to gleam with an otherworldly light. The disciples glimpse the risen and glorified Jesus, and they also see who they are becoming through him. Jesus is making them—making us—a new creation. Or, as Richard Rohr would put it, Jesus shows us the immortal diamond that we are as a function of our union with God.

Consider this passage from *Immortal Diamond*:

The Risen Christ is the standing icon of humanity in its final and full destiny. He is the pledge and guarantee of what God will do with all of our crucifixions. At last, we can meaningfully live with

---

1. "A Monologue from the Film *Kill Bill: Vol. 2* by Quentin Tarantino," Actorama, accessed June 13, 2017, http://www.actorama.com/ms/702/Quentin-Tarantino /Kill-Bill:-Vol.-2.

hope. It is no longer an absurd or tragic universe. Our hurts now become the home for our greatest hopes.[2]

On the Mount of the Transfiguration we get a glimpse of resurrection. But the way to the empty tomb always passes through the cross. And in the crucified Jesus, we see how God views us. On the cross Jesus embraces our agony and our loneliness. In him we see our own wounded hearts, shattered bodies, and lost hopes. We see our shame and fear, our regrets and sorrows. We see all of our crucifixions both great and small.

Some might say, "This doesn't describe me. I am successful. My hard work and smart choices have made me a winner. Sure, the world is full of losers, but I'm not one of them." Jesus has a reply. "Those who are well have no need of a physician, but those who are sick; I have come to call not the righteous but sinners to repentance."[3]

Whether we realize it or not, we all need the divine physician. Eventually a sword will pierce everyone's heart. A CT scan may show a mass in our kidney or a tumor in our child's brain. Our parent's amusing forgetfulness might prove to be the first signs of dementia. Epidemics, earthquakes, famines, and tornadoes don't really care how hard we work or how smart we are. We can't cure a friend's despair or defeat a loved one's addiction by being clever. Just in case you haven't noticed, everyone will eventually die. You can't dig your way out of the grave with shrewdness and industriousness.

Just as Jesus shows us how God views us, he also reveals God to us. On the cross Jesus reveals God's perfect compassion for us. And God's compassion is no mere affection. It is an irresistible power. Jesus' compassion turns death into life. To cite Rohr again, "The Crucified One is God's standing solidarity with the suffering, the tragedy, and the disaster of all time, and God's promise that it will not have the final word."[4]

---

2. Richard Rohr, *Immortal Diamond* (San Francisco, CA: Josey Bass, 2013). Kindle loc. 1377.

3. Luke 5:31–32.

4. Rohr, *Immortal Diamond*, Kindle loc. 2130

Jesus is how God views us. He sees us as the lost brought home. As the broken made whole. As the captive set free. Jesus finds us, mends us, and liberates us. He saves us by becoming one of us and making us one of his own.

Reflection Questions

1. What word, phrase, image, or idea in this chapter stood out to you? What ideas, stories, images, or questions did it suggest to you?
2. Does this chapter confirm, challenge, or enlarge your image of Jesus? Talk about how this is so for you.
3. This chapter says that Jesus is how God views us. What do you make of that? What do you think this calls you to do?
4. Like other chapters in part one of this book, this chapter discusses how our relationship with God in Christ makes us who we truly are in this life. That's part of what it means to be saved. Does this affirm or challenge how you've thought about being saved? How is God saving you right now?

Part Two

Retelling Your Story

I promise you that the discovery of your True Self will feel like a thousand pounds of weight have fallen from your back. You will no longer have to build, protect, or promote any idealized self-image. Living in the True Self is quite simply a much happier existence, even though we never live there a full twenty-four hours a day.

—Richard Rohr, *Immortal Diamond*

Find out who you are and do it on purpose.

—Dolly Parton

Chapter 6

Hearing Grace

Read Luke 17:11–19.

Grace has a way of sneaking up on us. Before we realize it, Jesus has been at work shaping us into his very own Body. We're just not able to see ourselves as he does yet.

I had a major surgery when I was in my early twenties. The surgeon prescribed months of postop rehab. As soon as possible, I showed up at the therapist's office. The woman who greeted me there eyed me warily and, with a chill in her voice, told me I would have to wait while she reviewed my file. Whatever it was I had been expecting from a therapist, this wasn't it. I realized that she was a speech therapist, not a psychological counselor. But I wasn't prepared for a harsh, uncaring taskmaster.

The spare waiting room lacked any decorations and its furnishings included half a dozen plain wooden chairs. For a miserably long half hour, my rear end grew increasingly numb and I struggled with the impulse to walk out. Just as I had formulated the perfect parting remark and decided to leave, the therapist emerged from her office with a softened expression and warmly invited me in. We sat across a small table from each other with a cassette player between us. Several big buttons formed the front of the device. One for play. Another for record. Rewind. Fast-forward. Stop.

She said, "You've been speaking without a soft palate for over twenty years. You've just had a major surgery to correct a speech impediment. Your pharyngeal flap will make it possible for you to make sounds that were physically impossible for you, like 's.' But you'll have to do exactly what I tell you to do."

This was pretty much what I had expected to hear. Life as I had always known it was a struggle to make myself understood. After all, I was born without the soft part of the roof of my mouth. As a toddler, I had received the first surgery designed to begin the repair of my birth defect. But the second surgery had never happened. I couldn't say "s" and badly garbled the letter "j." My speech was distressingly nasal.

My therapist continued, "You haven't heard yourself since the surgery, have you?" She reached for the cassette player. My heart froze. Speaking to others—anticipating the rejection and the ridicule and the assumptions about my low intelligence—was hard enough. Hearing a recording of my own nasal, garbled speech was torture.

"I can't do that," I told her. "I can't bear to hear myself like that."

She said evenly, "If you want to get better, you have to do this."

She said, "Just talk to me for a minute," and hit the record button.

For a couple of minutes I protested into the machine. She punched the stop button and said, "That's enough. Now listen carefully to this and we'll talk about it."

A voice I had never heard spoke to me from that little machine. It's the voice that I've come to recognize as my own.

"You don't need speech therapy," she said. "When you first came in, I assumed that you had a psychological problem. We get that here sometimes. People go to the wrong office. So I figured I had to get rid of you. But when I read your file, I realized that you just weren't able to hear your new voice yet."

I just wasn't able to hear my new voice yet. Even when we get a new life, it takes some time to know and accept who we've been made into.

A surgeon's skill had given me an entirely new life. A pharyngeal flap closed the airway from my voice box through my nose, mimicking what a normal palate does inside the mouth of most people. That's how we make sounds like "s" and "j." A scalpel in the hands of a professional had given me the mechanism for normal speech.

By what seems like a miracle, I used that new mechanism correctly with no instruction. Once the trauma from the surgery had subsided, my speech sounded like that of any normal Southern guy. I just wasn't able to hear it. In other words, knowing myself as a person with normal speech was going to take some time.

To put this another way, even after you've been healed, it can take a while to recognize and to accept yourself as a healed person. In my case, I had over two decades of living as an outsider. The surgical procedure had done nothing to remove my habits of defensiveness, fear, and loneliness. I still perceived myself as deformed and off-putting. I have to admit, when I read a story like Jesus' healing of the ten lepers, my own experience with healing influences my understanding of what's going on.

Jesus heals ten lepers. Only one comes back to say thank-you. Some teachers and preachers assume that the other nine lepers felt no gratitude. They went about their merry way without acknowledging Jesus' mercy. It may be that those nine lepers were a bunch of ingrates. But it could also be that they had grown so accustomed to feeling repulsive and to being shunned by their community that they continued viewing themselves as lepers. They just couldn't see their own smooth, healthy skin.

The risen Jesus gives all of us a new life. In Baptism he weaves us into his very own Body. The bread and the wine of Holy Eucharist gradually deepen our participation in his divine life. Jesus is changing us. Giving us a new life. But we just aren't able to see ourselves as he does yet.

We see this same pattern in Jesus' own life. After emerging from the tomb, the risen Jesus walked the earth for forty days. As Ronald Rolheiser explains, even Jesus had to get used to being a new creation.[1]

Grace sneaks up on us. It does its work on us before we even realize it. Our self-perception—and our perception of other people—lags

---

1. Ronald Rolheiser. *The Holy Longing: The Search for a Christian Spirituality* (New York: Image, 1998), 141–66.

behind the reality that Jesus is bringing about. Some of us will keep berating ourselves as jerks long after we've been forgiven. Even when our old wounds are nearly healed, we might struggle with kicking the habit of resentment. Some of us have been treated as outsiders for so long, we have trouble recognizing ourselves as the beloved children of God. But over time—through the power of the Sacraments, in the love of the community, in service to the poor and the marginalized—we begin to recognize and accept ourselves as the Body of Christ.

I would like to think that, in their own time, each of those nine lepers caught up with Jesus somewhere or other. They began to see themselves as he does. And that is when the real miracle happened for them. It's the real miracle that happens for us. We no longer see others though the lens of our old wounds and prejudices and fears. We begin to see others—especially strangers and foreigners—as Jesus does.

Reflection Questions

1. What word, phrase, image, or idea in this chapter stood out to you? What ideas, stories, images, or questions did it suggest to you?

2. Does this chapter bring an episode in your life into focus in a new way? Talk about how this is so for you. Does your new perspective on this event suggest a more gracious way to see yourself and to tell your life story?

3. This chapter says that grace has a way of sneaking up on us. Have you seen this happen to someone you know? Has it happened in your own life?

4. Do you struggle with telling your story a different way? Imagine how Jesus would tell your story. What do you hear?

Chapter 7

Forgiving Yourself

Read John 21:1–19.

"Some things can't be forgiven." Jim said these words as if he were reporting a fact so obvious as to be trivial. Judging from his tone, he might as well have said, "The sun rises in the east" or "Chickens lay eggs." It's the way things are. No point in discussing it any further.

It may sound paradoxical, but his resolutely flat delivery and emotionless tone conveyed a churning, barely contained menace and a gnawing despair. We were eating burgers at a pub near the church I was serving at the time. Jim had only just entered his twenties. He had the wiry, muscular frame of a wrestler in the lower weight classes. His black hair was a riot of uncombed locks shooting in all directions and tumbling over his forehead into his eyes. Those dark eyes were smoldering with unspoken judgment: "You're clueless."

Jim's parents were at wit's end. His drug and alcohol use worried them, but it was his frequent violence that moved them to ask me to speak with him. Night after night he would get wasted, capping most evenings with a brawl. If he didn't remember the fight, the fresh scrapes on his knuckles and the new bruises on his body told the tale plainly enough. He never struck his parents or his siblings. But he was perpetually irritable, verbally abusive, and predictably unpleasant to be around.

As you might imagine, I made all the referrals to the professionals that could work with Jim. And I was honest with his parents. Fixing Jim was way beyond my skill set. But I agreed to have lunch with him; to offer him my friendship as a formerly angry young man.

"So what do you mean?" I asked.

"I mean, some things can't be forgiven," he said.

"What sort of things are you not forgiving?"

I was expecting him to express anger toward his parents or an ex-girlfriend. Maybe an authority figure or a friend who had betrayed him. Instead, he said, "I don't have any trouble forgiving anybody. I've done things. Terrible things. They're not forgivable. I'm not forgivable."

I told him that I believe that God can and does forgive anything. I prepared to do some serious persuading about God's love for him. His response showed me that I had actually been completely clueless up to that point.

"I don't care," he said. "I don't want God's forgiveness. I know I don't deserve it. I'm unforgivable."

And that was that. End of the conversation as far as he was concerned. Clearly not one of my great pastoral success stories. And yet it was a significant learning experience for me.

Offering forgiveness can be wretchedly difficult. Conversely, accepting forgiveness can be just as profound a challenge as forgiving somebody else. As shorthand for the struggle to accept forgiveness, people will often talk about how hard it can be to forgive yourself. But I think this turn of phrase can be a little misleading. Our relief from the sins of our past comes not from within ourselves. It comes from beyond ourselves as a free gift.

When we forgive, we let go of grievances we have. Grievances can be hard to let go of, and we often pick them right back up again. The temptation to seek relief for our woundedness by blaming or harming another is very seductive. No wonder forgiving someone is often a long, uneven process.

Accepting forgiveness from another involves a different set of struggles. For starters, we have to admit not only that we have done something hurtful to someone, but that we cannot fix it or set things right. Admitting guilt for another person's sorrow or injury can be very painful. We are accountable, and yet we can do nothing to acquit ourselves. Oh, we might try to defend our actions by making excuses or to make up for what we've done through some future kindness, but we know that the future does not simply erase the past.

To be forgiven means to hear from the one we've injured, "I have let this go. I will not let what you have done stand between us." In other words, we have to put ourselves at someone else's mercy. We have to admit our powerlessness and to rely upon a power greater than ourselves to make us whole.

Even more difficult still, accepting forgiveness also means to take the first step toward reconciliation with the one we've injured. We do that by admitting that the hurtful thing we did was not just a one-off. Our wrongdoing arose from some deep, abiding flaw in our soul. And there we have the rub. To accept forgiveness, we have to submit ourselves to the transforming power of love. Yielding to love means to let go of what we have been and to embrace what love will make of us. In other words, to accept forgiveness means to stop trying to write the ending of our own story. Jesus writes an ending that will give new significance to every episode of our life. Even and especially those episodes that we assumed must diminish us or condemn us.

And that is exactly what the risen Jesus is doing with Peter on the shore of the Sea of Tiberias. Three times Jesus asks Peter, "Do you love me?" And three times Peter answers, "Yes." Jesus' three-fold question is not a coincidence. After Jesus had been arrested, Peter had denied his friend three times to save his own skin. Peter's awareness of this betrayal would have been quite a burden of guilt for him to carry. So Jesus teaches Peter, and teaches us, a lesson in accepting forgiveness.

Peter had been the brashest of the apostles. "I'll follow you even to death, Jesus! Even when all these slackers bail on you, I'll be right by your side." He was sure that his moral rectitude and spiritual depth would sustain him. His story was going to be a hero's tale. He would write the triumphant ending that tied everything together. And now, Peter had fallen on his face. All of his big talk highlighted and amplified the worst moment of his life. He had betrayed Jesus. So, he could take Judas's example and end it all. Or, he could admit his powerlessness. He couldn't see how he could write a noble ending after such a betrayal. And so he decided to let Jesus write it.

Consider how we read a novel or view a film. Through each scene we anticipate an ending that will reveal the significance of all that has come before. For instance, being stuck in an elevator or spilling a cup of coffee on a complete stranger can, in retrospect, become a crucial turning point in a love story. In Christ, none of us is defined by the worst moment of our lives or even what we take to be the best moments of our lives. The risen Jesus gives us a new life, makes us a new creation. New life in Christ transforms every episode of our lives. In Jesus' hands, even the events that make us wince with embarrassment and the ones that fill us with remorse become turning points in the story of our redemption.

We cannot write that ending for ourselves. Only Jesus can give us eternal life. We cannot know the details of life eternal. However, we can live our earthly life in anticipation of that redemptive ending. When we fall—and we will fall from time to time—we can rise in courageous confidence to take the next step. Jesus is risen. And he is raising us with him.

Reflection Questions

1. What word, phrase, image, or idea in this chapter stood out to you? What ideas, stories, images, or questions did it suggest to you?

2. Does this chapter bring an episode in your life into focus in a new way? Talk about how this is so for you. Does your new perspective on this event suggest a more gracious way to see yourself and to tell your life story?

3. Remember a time that you regretted what you did or said or failed to do. Did you receive forgiveness? Were you able to forgive yourself?

4. How do you tell the story of your past mistakes? Do you talk about regret or shame? Can you share an experience of the relief of being forgiven?

Chapter 8

Boiled Shrimp and Broken Toys

Read Luke 13:1–9.

After work one day Joy and I ran by Robbie G's to pick up some boiled shrimp for dinner. There's nothing fancy about Robby G's. Painted crawfish-red and tan, the flat-roofed building is surrounded by a parking lot that is mostly paved but partly gravel. The menu features Po Boys and fried seafood.

Having called ahead, Joy popped in for a couple of minutes. She returned to the car carrying a plastic bag filled with spiced, hot, freshly boiled shrimp. The aroma filled the car's tiny compartment. We hadn't gone more than ten feet before I realized that my bishop's vestments were hanging in the back seat. My blood pressure spiked as I imagined linen, wool, and silk absorbing the odor of boiled shrimp. The idea of reeking like a fish market on the coming Sunday lodged in the front of my mind. I hastily rolled down the windows and spent the rest of the drive home stewing and crabbing about what a terrible idea it was to bring pungent seafood into a small car transporting expensive, hard to clean, odor-absorbing vestments.

It's painful to remember such a hissy fit and even more embarrassing to admit out loud that I could have one. But that's not the whole story. For the rest of the evening I remained grumpy, and I woke up irritable the next morning. As I sat to reflect on scripture, to journal, and to pray silently, a memory welled up from some deep place.

I was about eight years old. Taylor and I were playing in my front yard. I had just gotten a new toy machine gun. Taking the toy gun, we climbed a tree next to the front porch and got on the roof. We pretended to fend off attackers for a while, then we decided to play some other game. As we started back down the tree, Taylor was holding the gun.

He said, "I'll just toss it down so I won't fall."

I said, "Don't do that—it'll break."

As he was letting go of the gun, he said, "Oh, it's not that far down."

The gun shattered. He said, "No big deal. Just tape it back together."

It's not surprising that I felt the loss of the new toy or that the carelessness of my playmate made me mad fifty years ago. The spiritual news flash for me was that as an adult I still resented an eight-year-old boy for being, well, an eight-year-old boy.

Jesus was reminding me that he is actively tending my life, nurturing it and pruning it to bear the fruit of a holy soul. And that's what Jesus is doing for all of us. Jesus does not guarantee a favorable set of outward circumstances. Health and wealth elude millions of deeply faithful people around the world and around the corner. Faith in Jesus does not shield us from pain and sorrow, tragedy and violence.

We hear of heartbreak in the news on a daily basis: an Uber driver in Michigan on a random shooting spree; a perpetrator in Kansas opening fire at his former workplace, having taken aim at complete strangers on his way to the final crime scene. As Jesus said of those slaughtered by Pilate in the midst of worship and of those who died when a tower in Jerusalem collapsed, "Were these people any worse sinners than anybody else?"[1] In other words, Jesus is discrediting what was then a common theology. Some believed that when bad things happened to people, it was God's way of singling them out as sinners. Bad things, they thought, happened to bad people. Correlatively, good

---

1. Luke 13:2b (paraphrase).

things happen to good people. That's just not how God operates. In Jesus we see that God is intimately involved in our lives. We're all up to our eyeballs in the messiness of human life. And Jesus dives right in to nurture us into holiness.

And yet, Jesus goes on to say, "Unless you repent, you will all perish just as they did."[2] Jesus is not contradicting himself. Instead, he's helping us understand how we are accountable under the reign of God's grace. In Jesus, God is wholly invested in each of our lives. Jesus tends us and nurtures us. The fruit that we bear is not what we achieve or our outward circumstances or status. The fruit we bear is who we become. In my case, Jesus is freeing me from an old pattern of responding to hurt and betrayal and rejection with resentment. In place of resentment, Jesus is growing a forgiving soul in me.

Soul work is what Jesus had in mind when he told the parable of the fig tree.[3] A certain fig tree wasn't bearing fruit, and the owner of the vineyard wanted to cut it down. The gardener asked for a little extra time to nurture the tree, believing that with the right care it would yield succulent figs. The values and assumptions of our cultural context can prevent us from getting Jesus' point here. We live in an achievement-obsessed society. We judge others and ourselves on the basis of the results we produce. So, when we hear that the tree must bear fruit or be struck down, we hear Jesus saying that God will focus on our moral and spiritual achievements. It's as if God is using a checklist to grade our behavior. But the fruit that Jesus has in mind is not merely how well we follow the rules and how regularly we say our prayers. God is concerned with who we become. And who we become stretches into eternity.

Consider the case of two people facing very similar sets of circumstances. One person resists Jesus' nurturing love. That person clings to resentments or contempt or indifference or greed, and the increasingly lonely, narrow, hollow soul he or she inhabits on earth will become that person's infinitely cold, isolated dwelling place for all

2. Luke 13:5.
3. Luke 13:6–9.

of eternity. The time on earth will have become the beginning of hell. Even the fleeting joys of this brief life will fade into regret.

A second person yields to Jesus' loving hand. Resentment turns to forgiveness. Contempt and indifference to compassion. Greed to generosity. Resting in God and bound to the well-being of our neighbor, this second person glimpses heaven already in the changes and the chances of this planet. The two people experience similar life circumstances and yet their eternal trajectories are radically different. That difference lies in their openness to the nurturing power of divine love.

Boiled shrimp and broken toys may not seem the stuff of spiritual transformation. But they are the stuff of ordinary life. And ordinary life is where we'll find Jesus tending our soul.

Reflection Questions

1. What word, phrase, image, or idea in this chapter stood out to you? What ideas, stories, images, or questions did it suggest to you?

2. Does this chapter bring an episode in your life into focus in a new way? Talk about how this is so for you. Does your new perspective on this event suggest a more gracious way to see yourself and to tell your life story?

3. When you're faced with adversity and disappointment, do you respond with blame and resentment? What story do you think you're telling about yourself that leads to these emotions? Can you imagine a different story?

4. Can you tell a gracious story about times you have overreacted or sulked? How do events like this fit into the larger story of a person growing in love and grace?

Chapter 9

Restoring Our Sanity

Read Luke 19:1–10.

Honestly, sometimes I just lose my mind. I hear things that nobody is saying. For instance, Joy came back from her usual morning walk with our six-month-old Lab-mix, Gracie. Gracie was ecstatic. Joy, not so much.

"Ugh. She was awful," Joy said. "She kept jumping up for treats. And her stomach is completely off."

I heard, "She's never been like this before. If you hadn't been sharing your popcorn with her yesterday, she wouldn't be like this."

My first response was to think, "Thank goodness she didn't catch me feeding her the Wheat Thins." Then I just shut down. Or, more accurately, I spiraled down with a crazy story about what was happening: Joy is blaming me for her lousy walk with the dog. How dare she blame me! Oh really, so she's just going to offload her frustrations on me. Well I'm just not going to take it.

I went from relief at not being caught slipping Wheat Thins to Gracie to full-blown breakfast-table sulk in light speed. Our daughter, Meredith, chatted merrily away as I stared glumly into my mango Greek yogurt. Joy looked on warily. Once back in our room, Joy said, "You want to tell me what's going on?"

Joy realizes that this is the first step in a dance she has had to do with me from time to time. It's called, "Getting Jake to Step Back from the Abyss." We did it much more often when we were younger. It's fairly rare these days, but Joy is clear about how it works. "I'd rather not say," is followed by, "How could you talk to me like that," to a grudging admission, "Right, actually, that's not what you really said. It's what I heard."

Usually I'm tired or overfunctioning, frustrated or anxious. My spiritual batteries are low. That's when I seem most likely to hear rotten stories about me. I attribute those stories to her or to someone else. But the truth is, they are false, toxic stories I'm telling about myself. In essence, they all say the same thing. You're not enough: smart enough, capable enough, fit enough. Fill in the blank in front of "enough" however you like. The result is the same. Life is about measuring up, and I don't. All my little crazy, self-condemning stories belong on the judgment shelf of my interior library. Joy gently walks me to the grace section of that library by simply hanging in there with me. Her persistent love nudges me toward getting the story right.

Every story that Jesus tells about us starts with our being his beloved. That's the story each of us needs to learn about ourselves. And when that's the story we tell, how we behave toward others changes. As the beloved, we can genuinely love even the unlovely. We do remarkable things. We accept our imperfect selves. We forgive those who injure us. We make amends to those we've injured. We show compassion and generosity to strangers and even to those who hate us. In other words, salvation happens.

That's the kind of salvation we see when Jesus encounters Zacchaeus. Jesus is passing through Jericho. Throngs of people press in to get a glimpse of him. Zacchaeus lacks the height to see over the crowds, so he scrambles up a tree for a better view. Zacchaeus is a chief tax collector. That means he's in management. The people who collect the taxes report to him. Being in the tax collection business meant that you were collaborating with the Roman occupiers. In other words, Zacchaeus had a lousy reputation in Jericho.

We don't know any details about what Zacchaeus was like before meeting Jesus. We don't know why he wanted to see Jesus. And we certainly don't know what stories he told himself about himself. But we do know that meeting Jesus changed him. Jesus characterized it this way. "Today salvation has come to this house." Luke Timothy Johnson suggests a slightly different translation of that line: Today salvation happened in this house.[1] Salvation is something that is happening. In our day-to-day lives. In small ways and big ways. Again and again.

In Jesus' culture, sharing a meal with someone brought you into an enduring personal relationship. By eating with Zacchaeus, Jesus was saying, "I am your friend. You are my beloved." Contrary to what you might expect from a Roman collaborator, Zacchaeus committed himself to compassion and working for justice. He would give away half of his possessions to the poor.

It takes courage to listen to the grievances others have against you. Zacchaeus committed to hearing those grievances and to restoring relationship with his neighbors. Salvation was happening that day. And the next day. And the next day. Stretching into eternity. Salvation, you see, is about who we are becoming, not just where we are heading after we die.

Some Christians narrowly define salvation in terms of our final destination. Being saved means to avoid hell and to get into heaven. Eternal life means to spend forever in paradise. No pain. No sorrow. Endless golf or tennis or fishing. In other words, all play and no work. In brief, eternal life is all about your address in the next life. Location is everything.

By contrast, Jesus teaches us that eternal life is a way of living. That way of living derives from our relationship with Christ. Jesus imparts his life to us, saturates us with his life. Jesus gave us the Holy Eucharist to show us what all of life is meant to be. In some mysterious way we partake of him; we participate in his very life. In the bread and the wine, we see the Body of Christ. When we partake of it, we become what we have beheld. We become the Body of Christ. Salvation happens.

What the Sacrament shows us liturgically happens in ways mundane and profound every day. We sit with the awkward kid at lunch

---

1. See his translation in *Sacra Pagina: The Gospel of Luke* (Collegeville, MN: Liturgical Press, 1991).

and his and our loneliness abates. Tensions dissolve with a colleague over a cup of coffee. Sitting quietly with a grieving friend brings solace to us both. We feed the hungry and find contentment. Shelter the homeless and feel security. Ensuring access to health care for everyone we realize a new depth of human dignity. Petting the dog at the end of a trying day, we remember the basic goodness of the Creation.

Salvation is happening in such moments. Jesus is working through us, making us more like him. From time to time, we all lose our minds. And Jesus restores us to sanity. Salvation happens.

Reflection Questions

1. What word, phrase, image, or idea in this chapter stood out to you? What ideas, stories, images, or questions did it suggest to you?
2. Does this chapter bring an episode in your life into focus in a new way? Talk about how this is so for you. Does your new perspective on this event suggest a more gracious way to see yourself and to tell your life story?
3. In this chapter the author says that salvation happens in our day-to-day lives. Tell the story about a time in your life when you experienced salvation happening or, in retrospect, you can see that it was happening.
4. Do you carry within you the toxic stories that other people have told about something you did or said or didn't do? Recall that event as clearly as you can. Retell that story as if you were Jesus talking about a beloved friend.

Chapter 10

Stretching Each Other

Read Hebrews 12:18–29.

When I fully owned the truth that my father had physically and emotionally battered my mother, I was liberated from my deep need for his approval. For decades I had labored—mostly unwittingly—to win his attention and his respect. My sense of worth hinged on getting the applause that I assumed would surely come with the next achievement, award, or promotion. Then one day my stepsister sent me a letter outlining my father's abusive relationship with *her* mother. My stepsister had had a fierce conflict with him about his treatment of her mother, and she reached out to me in solidarity. Her words forced me to recognize that my father's violence toward my mother was not a momentary lapse in character. Rather, it arose from a deeply engrained habit of using intimidation and coercion to get his way. This was a man from whom I could expect only manipulation and condescension.

This dismal and painful epiphany about my father led me to reexamine the source of my own sense of identity. To be honest, I didn't want to define myself—and I didn't want anyone else to define me—as an abusive father's son. Eventually, I came to see that, first and foremost, I am a child of God. And this insight led me to admit, at least intellectually, that everybody else is a child of God, too. But you know, seeing yourself as a child of God doesn't happen in a single instant, and seeing everybody else that way can feel like an impossibly tall order. Each person is a complex and textured reality. Every time we genuinely seek to understand another person, we get stretched in ways that we didn't anticipate. And it is precisely this kind of stretching that prepares us to encounter divine reality in its fullness. But I'm getting ahead of myself.

A couple of years ago, I connected with my half-brother's daughter and my half-sister's daughter. (Yes, this is a very complex family system. My father was married three times. Just roll with me.) *My* father was, of course, *their* grandfather. The man they knew was kind and generous. Doting and supportive. The very same man who had paid no child support for me paid for braces and the like for them. That kindness toward his granddaughters is the sort of thing I would like to do if I get to be a grandfather someday. It really is admirable and generous.

Facing this aspect of my father's character changed who I am. Again. My heart was uncomfortably stretched. I realize that I don't get to reduce anyone to the story I can tell about the rotten things they've done to me and to people I love. Okay, I'm still struggling with this, but at least I pull myself back from the brink when I start to think the worst of another person. Each person's story begins and ends with this truth: he or she is a child of God. Even my father.

Maybe someday no one I meet will stretch my ability to recognize the dignity of every human being. My heart is not yet that expansive. Some people still press my buttons, get on my last nerve, and make me reach for an extra dose of blood pressure medication. And in each of these encounters God seeks to expand my soul just a bit more.

God apparently recognizes that our souls can only take so much stretching at one time. Too much reality blows your mind. Explodes your heart. Scorches your soul. God's ultimate goal is to share the fullness of the divine self with us. God is way more than any of us can handle all at once. That's what the writer of Hebrews is getting at when he says, "Our God is a consuming fire."[1] God is perfect, infinite, unrelenting love and beauty and goodness.

---

1. Hebrews 12:29.

Think of the "Wow!" you utter at a sunset and magnify that by a gazillion times. It would be like touching your eyeball to the surface of the sun. Paradoxically, we yearn for that vision, and yet we're just not ready for it. You may remember that Moses asked to see God. Moses got his wish, but only in a way that God figured he could handle. God instructed Moses to hide in a cleft of a rock. And even then, God gave Moses only the briefest glimpse of the divine backside.[2]

In the life after this life, we will be in God's nearer presence. Great theologians like Thomas Aquinas teach us that we will enjoy the beatific vision: the direct self-communication of God to our souls. The beatific vision is our ultimate happiness. God created each of us to yearn for this perfect, uninterrupted union with our Maker. But as we are right now, a direct encounter with the fullness of God would be a massive overload for our souls. It would be more than we could bear. God would be a consuming fire. We need lots of stretching before we're ready for such an intimate encounter with the holy.

As it turns out, God is getting us ready in a myriad of ways. For instance, in the Blessed Sacrament we receive the very Body of Christ. We are becoming what we receive. Beauty inhabits nature and art. Our encounters with the finite beauty of starry skies and fragrant blooms, Mary Cassatt's paintings, and Mozart's concertos expand our hearts and imaginations in preparation for God's infinite Beauty. Most challenging and tender of all is other people. Everyone we meet is created in the image of God. Every cranky toddler and grumpy uncle, every preening athlete and lumpy couch potato, every hardened felon and struggling addict walking this planet is a child of God. When we respect the dignity of those who most tempt us to flee or to strike out, to judge or to ignore, our souls grow in their capacity to receive the gift of God's own presence.

People, in all our fierce complexity and tender contradictions, are children of God. Our Maker has given us to each other to love and understand each other. That turns out to be quite a stretch. But loving

2. Exodus 33:18–34:9.

each other is precisely the stretching we need to make room in ourselves for the divine Love itself.

Reflection Questions

1. What word, phrase, image, or idea in this chapter stood out to you? What ideas, stories, images, or questions did it suggest to you?
2. Does this chapter bring an episode in your life into focus in a new way? Talk about how this is so for you. Does your new perspective on this event suggest a more gracious way to see yourself and to tell your life story?
3. Have you ever changed your mind about how you see another person? What happened in your life to bring you to that new perspective?
4. When we see another person from a different perspective, we sometimes see ourselves in a new way. Talk about a time that this happened for you. This can also happen in the opposite way. We see ourselves differently, so we get a different take on another person. Have you had this experience?

Part Three

Family, Friends, and Other Strangers

I'm beginning to think that maybe it's not just how much you love someone. Maybe what matters is who you are when you're with them.
—Anne Tyler, *The Accidental Tourist*

Chapter 11

Being Normal
Almost Killed Me

R*ead Matthew* 3:1–12.

"I used to be normal." John pushed his words out two or three at a time, as if someone were turning an mp3 file on and off at haphazard intervals. You could see the strain in his jaw and throat during each unintended break in his speech.

We were sharing a bench in a Greyhound bus station in Greenville, South Carolina. I had observed John's palsied gait as he had approached where I was sitting. He had struck up a conversation as soon as he had sat down.

"What are you doing here dressed like that?"

I was eighteen and a senior at St. Pius X Catholic High School in Atlanta. We had just run in the Furman Relays' meet, and my track team had left me behind. I was wearing my track uniform. And, yes, it was more than a little awkward.

"Well, my dad and his new wife came up from rural Georgia to watch me run. I joined them in their car after the meet to wait out a rainstorm. My team thought he was giving me a ride, so they left. He didn't feel like adding an hour to his trip, so he gave me bus money and dumped me off here."

We chatted for a few more minutes, then he said, "I used to be normal."

John stood a few inches over six feet. His broad shoulders narrowed to a thin waist. Thick black hair and a square jaw framed his face. A motorcycle crash had scrambled his brain. He would never speak or walk the way he once had. He said, "I'm not normal anymore" like he was telling me that he had had a grilled cheese sandwich for lunch. There was no hint of regret, frustration, or self-pity in his voice. He was just reporting a mundane fact.

Horrified, I blurted out something like, "Don't say that! Of course you're normal. You're like all the rest of us. I can understand you just fine." As I recall, he looked at me like I was missing something pretty obvious. In truth, I was. And that truth was about me, not him.

I was dying to be normal. Or at least, I was dying to make people think I was normal. Normal people get acceptance and love. Abnormal people eat alone in the lunch room. I knew the truth. I wasn't normal at all. But I sure wanted to pass as normal.

You see, I was born with a cleft palate. When I was eighteen, it hadn't been fully corrected, so I was saddled with a terrible speech impediment. A student in a Catholic school filled with big, happy, intact families, my parents were divorced. And my dad almost never showed up. I lived with my mom and her parents. My mom and my grandparents were immigrants from Austria who had passed through Ellis Island following the Second World War. We ate brown bread and knockwurst while everybody else in the neighborhood had fried chicken and cornbread for supper. English was obviously not the primary language in our house. I wasn't normal. I never even used to be normal. And trying to look like it was killing me.

I now realize that it wasn't being abnormal that was crushing me. Instead, my spiritual arrhythmia arose from the all-too-human game of separating people into neat boxes of normal and abnormal. We have a tendency to make ourselves feel significant by finding somebody to be better than. When we're better than somebody else, we get the thrill of feeling superior to be sure. But we also find an easy target to blame for what's going wrong in our own lives.

As a bishop in the Episcopal Church, it saddens me to admit that from time to time religious institutions play the normal-abnormal game. And we've broken hearts and crushed souls along the way. By contrast, Jesus came to make clear that God doesn't see human beings in these terms. Jesus—especially the infant Jesus—shows us just what humans look like to God: fragile, vulnerable, and needy. We wither unless nurtured. We thrive only by being connected.

The tendency of religious institutions to crush souls with the normal-abnormal game compelled John the Baptist to blast the religious leaders of his day. Big crowds had gathered to hear him in the desert. He called out to them to prepare for the Kingdom of Heaven. By heaven he doesn't mean what people frequently mean today: a paradise that awaits us after death. The Kingdom of Heaven is this world, only this world transformed and renewed by God's loving reign. And then he spots the Pharisees and calls them a brood of vipers. In John the Baptist's view, these religious authorities think of themselves as the standard of normal. They believe that their moral rectitude and their religious observances give them a passing grade with God. And their status entitles them to say who lands in the normal box and who gets tossed in the misfit pile.

Jesus shows us that God doesn't scrutinize us from a distance to make sure we're normal. God seeks us out in all our squalid, tender, sordid, beautiful quirkiness—each and every one of us. Trying to be normal will kill you. It nearly killed me. God draws us to something better: being God's beloved. Recognizing that everyone else is God's beloved too. There is nothing normal about that.

Reflection Questions

1. What word, phrase, image, or idea in this chapter stood out to you? What ideas, stories, images, or questions did it suggest to you?

2. Does this chapter make you think of someone you dislike or fear? Someone you judge or resent or harbor a grievance against? Someone you envy or blame or simply can't connect with? Talk about the events that led you to this perspective. Now imagine how Jesus would tell this person's story as his beloved friend.

3. Do you try to seem normal? If so, talk about a time you were trying to be normal? If not, tell the story about how you learned to let go of the idea of being normal.
4. Talk about a time when you saw another person from a completely different perspective.

Chapter 12

Ugly Love

R*ead Luke* 7:36–8:3

Cheryl Strayed used to write an advice column at *The Rumpus*[1] called "Dear Sugar." Her readers knew her only by her alias. The messages to Sugar usually came with their own aliases for public consumption. Some signed with a single letter like "M." Other pseudonyms expressed the challenge, the heartache, or the chaos about which the writer was seeking counsel.

Strayed's book *Tiny Beautiful Things* gathers together some especially poignant and vivid exchanges in her column. Most of them touch me and move me (and sometimes bewilder me and even unsettle me). One writer's story—and the response that Strayed gave him—has stayed lodged in my head and my heart. The author called himself Beast with a Limp.[2]

Born with a blood disorder, Beast's body is visibly lopsided. One side appears normal while the other is withered and contorted. Honestly assessing his pronounced deformities and obvious disfigurements, he calls himself an ugly, broken man. His words convey no hint of self-loathing or self-pity, just realistic acceptance. While Beast with a Limp has many friends, the special intimacy of romance has evaded

---

1. http://therumpus.net.
2. Cheryl Strayed, *Tiny Beautiful Things* (New York: Vintage Books, 2012). See "Beauty and the Beast," 149–50.

51

him. He writes Sugar with a simple, blunt question. Should he cling to the hope of finding that special kind of love with someone else, or should he set aside that hope as a fruitless, demoralizing fantasy? Who, after all, would want to be embraced by, to be kissed by, to be caressed by his repulsive form?

Most of us inhabit bodies that fall into the normal range of appearance. We might not like how our butts look in jeans or wish our abs looked more like a washboard than a washtub. Our noses may seem to us big and our lips thin. Maybe the first word that comes to mind when we stand naked in front of the mirror is sagging, not tight. No matter, we're in the broad part of the bell curve when it comes to our looks. And for many of us, that still doesn't quiet our fears.

Most of us have some story about ourselves or a hidden desire or a favorite fantasy that we keep caged in the darkest recesses of our hearts. It's our Beast. We're sure that exposing the beast would bring humiliation and rejection. And so we keep the beast out of sight. Frequently, we keep the beast hidden from ourselves. And when we spot the beast in somebody else, we are quick to call for its annihilation or its expulsion or its immediate transformation.

Jesus has the uncanny, disconcerting ability to see through appearances. To see what we take to be our repulsive Beast. When some people talk about the holiness of God, they say that sin is so repugnant to holiness that it cannot even approach the divine. God would never tolerate a sinner's embrace, kiss, or caress. In other words, most of us are out of luck if we're looking for intimacy with God in the lumpy stew that is our daily lives.

And yet, Luke tells us the story of Jesus and the sinful woman at the Pharisee's dinner party. All the guests have reclined at the host's table. Don't think about your own dinner table. Diners back then lay on the floor with their heads propped on an elbow facing a low table. Their feet were stretched away from the table. That's why the nameless sinful woman could kneel easily at Jesus' feet. She washed and caressed and kissed and anointed his feet and even dried them with her hair. Now, this woman's actions seem more than a little intimate to me.

In disdain for Jesus and the woman, the Pharisee thought, "If he knew what a low life this woman was, Jesus wouldn't put up with this. Street walker! Some prophet!" The irony is that Jesus reads people in a way that only God can. We linger on appearances. Make assumptions about what we see on the surface. Draw conclusions from only brief observations. Jesus sees the whole picture of our lives and the deepest chambers of our hearts. And he welcomes this sinful woman's embrace.

Jesus knows this woman better than she knows herself. And he knows the Pharisee. He sees the contempt, the spiritual condescension, and the political animosity. And yet he breaks bread with a man who despises him and dishonors him by withholding even the most basic gestures of hospitality. The Pharisee thinks himself too morally put together to suffer this woman's touch. Her very presence— to say nothing of her kiss and her caress—threatens to undo him. He withholds himself from her to prevent his own disintegration. Paradoxically, by keeping this woman at a safe distance, the Pharisee erects a barrier between himself and the God who showed up at his very own dinner table.

The Pharisee suffers the delusion that his moral rectitude has made him presentable to God. His only challenge in this life is to retain the moral integrity he has already achieved and to point out to others how far short of the mark they still are.

The sinful woman has no such illusion. She realizes that we all fall—all of us—and we cannot rise on our own. Only God can bring us to our feet again. And in so doing, God makes us more than we were before we fell.

Jesus puts it like this: "Her sins, which were many, have been forgiven; hence she has shown great love."[3] She recognizes that she has fallen, that she will likely fall again, and that God is there to raise her up anew. She has compassion for everyone else who falls. She's been there. She will not withhold her embrace from any of the fallen people she meets in the streets or the alleys, bars, and dives of her life, for that

---

3. Luke 7:47.

is where she will embrace the living God. God's love for her liberates her to love as best she can, even while she's still coming to terms with the beast that rattles around in her soul. By contrast, the Pharisee's obsession with his own integrity incarcerates him in a loveless cell of self-righteous judgment.

Cheryl Strayed's advice to Beast with a Limp was simple and harrowing. The problem isn't that other people might not love you. Of course some people will reject you or be indifferent to you. The problem is your fear of being hurt. Love means being vulnerable. And being vulnerable takes courage. Never give up on being loved. And for those of us who have encountered Christ in some guise or other, we can say this, "Never forget that you are loved." That is why you can love much.

Reflection Questions

1. What word, phrase, image, or idea in this chapter stood out to you? What ideas, stories, images, or questions did it suggest to you?
2. Does this chapter make you think of someone you dislike or fear? Someone you judge or resent or harbor a grievance against? Someone you envy or blame or simply can't connect with? Talk about the events that led you to this perspective. Now imagine how Jesus would tell this person's story as his beloved friend.
3. Think about a person that you think is ugly, awkward, or off-putting. Now look for something beautiful, graceful, and attractive about him or her. Imagine how Jesus would describe this person.
4. Think about someone who has a negative view of you, especially someone who is likely to cling to that point of view. What do you know about this person that might lead her or him to tell such a negative story?

Chapter 13

Not Those People

Read Luke 10:25–37.

The bell marking the end of recess had rung ten minutes earlier. Most of our fourth grade classmates had already clambered up the old metal fire escape that gave access from the playground to our second-story classroom. A few of us routinely lagged behind. We squeezed every microsecond of play we could from the school day. This time we had lingered too long, and we knew it. We bolted up those rusty steps. But as I got to the landing by our doorway, I heard other kids still on the playground.

Turning around, I spotted boys and girls who seemed to belong to several different grade levels. There were elementary school kids and middle schoolers mixed in with high schoolers. Some moved awkwardly. Others stood idly watching nothing in particular. There was lots of laughter and running about, much the same as you would have seen watching my class.

I said to the guy behind me, "Who are those kids?"

"Those are the retards," he said.

I didn't know what a retard was. And yet, I realized that my classmate had hurled that word like an insult. This was decades before I came to understand how disrespectful and offensive this word is. But even then I gathered that nobody wanted to be one and that we should consider ourselves better than those people. They were the outcasts, the underclass. That's when I saw Tony playing with those people.

Three years earlier, on my first day of first grade at Louisville Academy, my mother had brought me into the classroom. We were late. All the other kids were seated at their places in wooden chairs along the sides of wooden tables. I didn't know a soul, and the teacher honestly looked like the Wicked Witch of the West. Despite every effort to keep it together, I broke into uncontrollable sobs. From somewhere toward the back of the room, another boy got up and walked to the front. He put his arm around me. "I'll be your friend. Come sit next to me." That was Tony.

Midway through second grade, I spotted Tony cheating on our weekly spelling test. Our teacher had noticed as well. She swept down the aisle, grabbed him by the hand, and disappeared with him for some time. She returned alone with no explanation. I didn't see Tony again until that day on the fire escape two years later. Now he was no longer one of us. He was one of those people. They belonged over there. We belonged over here with our kind of people. If you mixed with those people, your friends might start to think that you're one of them. Best to keep them at a distance.

Jesus talked a lot about those people. Or, more accurately, Jesus taught again and again that our tendency to divide people into us and them, higher and lower, insider and outsider, bore absolutely no resemblance to the Kingdom of God. The last will be first and the first will be last. Those who exalt themselves will be humbled and the humble will be exalted. The meek shall inherit the earth.

We see those people. We see the losers, the outsiders, the clueless, and the tacky. God doesn't see things that way. And that's a problem. So Jesus uses one of those people to teach us a lesson about being one of his people. He tells the parable of the Good Samaritan.

To get your head around Jesus' meaning, you have to understand that a Good Samaritan was like a healthy leper. In the Jewish mind of the day, there was no such thing. Samaritans were no-good half-breeds. After the Assyrians had conquered the Northern Kingdom of Israel around 722 BCE, they pursued a policy of cultural annihilation. They scattered the Northern Kingdom's inhabitants into foreign lands and forced intermarriage with non-Jews. The Samaritans were the product. For Southern Kingdom folk, the Samaritans were tainted. Inferior stock.

So it's no accident that Jesus chooses a Samaritan to teach a pious Talmud lawyer a lesson in what it means to love your neighbor as yourself. To catch Jesus in blasphemy or some other form of heresy, the lawyer had asked, "How do I get eternal life?" Quick on his feet, Jesus responded with a question that a self-proclaimed Bible expert couldn't resist. "What does scripture say?"

Forgetting that the whole point of asking Jesus a question in the first place was to catch Jesus saying something incriminating, the lawyer blurted out the summary of the law. His desire to be the guy who knew the right answer got the best of him. "Love God right down to your gizzard and love your neighbor like your life depended on it."

That's when one of those moment-of-clarity things happened. The lawyer realized that he loved Jesus—and probably a long list of what he considered those people—slightly less than an earache. So, he quickly justified himself with another question. "Who is my neighbor?" In other words, "Who really counts as my neighbor? Who do I have to love and who can I count as *those* people?"

And so Jesus tells this parable about a Samaritan who comes across a wounded Jew in a ditch. The Jew represented a whole class of people who had been condescending to and discriminating against the Samaritan for his whole life. The Jew was no friend to the Samaritan. And yet the Samaritan showed him friendship. Instead of seeing one of those people, the Samaritan saw an equal. He saw an *equal*. He did not condescend to someone less than himself. Even thinking of someone as less fortunate is a way of making them one of those people. Instead, the Samaritan showed compassion. In compassion, we stand in solidarity with someone in their weakness and need. We can do that only when we recognize ourselves as weak and needy, and then listen to the stories that others have to tell.

Being a neighbor means to listen. Not just to people like us. But to the people God has literally placed around us. If, because of their social class or race, we see them as those people and keep a safe distance from them, we are refusing to be a neighbor. Jesus doesn't instruct us to wait and see who qualifies as our neighbor. With the parable of the Good Samaritan, Jesus sends us into the world to be neighbors to everyone we meet.

That's what Tony did with me. He wouldn't allow me to remain a stranger, to be one of those people. He didn't worry about my race or my social class or my country of origin. Tony saw my fear and my loneliness. He knew what that was like. So, he put his arm around me. And he said, "I'll be your friend." He treated me as his neighbor.

Reflection Questions

1. What word, phrase, image, or idea in this chapter stood out to you? What ideas, stories, images, or questions did it suggest to you?

2. Does this chapter make you think of someone you dislike or fear? Someone you judge or resent or harbor a grievance against? Someone you envy or blame or simply can't connect with? Talk about the events that led you to this perspective. Now imagine how Jesus would tell this person's story as his beloved friend.

3. Have you ever been the stranger or the outsider in a social situation? Talk about what that was like. What stories were others telling about you? What assumptions were they making about you? What stories were you telling about them?

4. Are there parts of town you avoid? What stories are you telling about the people who live there? Now imagine the story that Jesus is telling about them.

Chapter 14

Walls and Bridges

*R*ead Genesis 15:1–12, 17–18.

Mike threw a rock and hit me in the face at the corner of my eye. The jagged little piece of granite missed the eyeball itself by a scant millimeter. We had been walking down a country road with a group of boys. Mike had been several steps behind me. I had been turning around to say something to him. The rock struck me just as Mike was coming into view. Dazed by the pain and stunned by the sudden impact, I stooped with hands on knees for a few minutes. Mike was frantic, apologizing. Saying again and again that it was an accident.

He and I had been good friends for years. I was eleven. Mike was just a bit younger. He was a gentle boy, given to kindness and quick to cry when his feelings were injured. He was crying now because he had hurt me. As if someone had flipped a switch in my head, my initial shock gave way to a blinding fury. I let go a barrage of accusatory, mean-spirited words, insisting that Mike had purposely hit me with that rock. I stormed home and wouldn't speak to Mike for weeks.

I built an emotional wall around me that utterly excluded Mike. Time might have dismantled that wall given the chance. Grace might have nudged my heart toward forgiveness and understanding. But my mother and I moved away from that town later that summer. The wall that I built in fear and anger and pain—from my own need to seek comfort by placing blame on someone else—left me with the enduring memory of a friendship fractured by my own failure to forgive.

That's quite a contrast to what we witnessed in Charleston, South Carolina, in June of 2015. A twenty-one-year-old man had entered an AME church and murdered nine people with whom he had just finished a Bible study. He had hoped to start a race war. Instead, in a Charleston courtroom, some of the victims' family members forgave the shooter, prayed for his soul, and encouraged him to repent.[1] They walked across a bridge of compassion toward him, urging him to join them. Those individuals could trust that bridge to support them, because it was a bridge not of their own making. Jesus erected that bridge. In Jesus, God heals our own injured souls and mends the shattered relationships between us.

Jesus dismantles walls and builds bridges. That's part of what we mean when we say that Jesus is our savior. He dismantles the walls we erect and builds bridges to span the fissures and gaps between the divine heart and the human heart, between human heart and human heart.

We don't have to do anything to persuade Jesus to be about this work. It's how he rolls. That's just who he is. But to experience the relationships that Jesus seeks to restore, we have to stop adding new bricks to the walls Jesus tears down. And we have to step out onto the bridge that Jesus is building. In other words, we have to believe. The story of Abraham teaches us precisely this lesson.

Abram—before God changed his name to Abraham—was already old as dirt. So was his wife, Sarai (soon to be renamed Sarah). God had long ago promised Abram offspring, with the emphasis on "long ago." God is taking an uncomfortably long time to make good on that promise, and Abram is beginning to waver in his confidence. God renews the promise and Abram takes God's word for it. Genesis puts it this way, "He believed the LORD; and the LORD reckoned it to him as righteousness."[2]

---

1. Mark Berman, "'I Forgive You': Relatives of Charleston Church Shooting Victims Address Dylann Roof," *Washington Post*, June 19, 2015, https://www .washingtonpost.com/news/post-nation/wp/2015/06/19/i-forgive-you-relatives -of-charleston-church-victims-address-dylann-roof/?utm_term=.48249cb3ea9f.
2. Genesis 15:6.

If all you hear in this story is that God promised Abram a son and that God would give Abram what he wanted so long as he believed in the promise, you will miss the point. Abram is agreeing to keep making his own life all about God's redeeming mission on earth.

God initially called Abram out of his hometown of Ur in order to make him and Sarai the founders of a new tribe. God sought to work through this new tribe to bless all the tribes of the earth.[3] Abram wanted an heir. But he also understood that his life—and the life of his eventual descendants—would be instrumental in bridging the gaps that divide God's many children. Abram gave himself to that divine bridge-building project.

God completes this reconciling work with the hands and feet of Jesus. As it turns out, we are those hands and feet. Believing in Jesus is much more than assenting to a list of theological concepts. We clarify our beliefs with Creeds, doctrines, and prayers, but our belief is real when we act—when we act as Jesus has taught us to act.

We believe in Jesus when we forgive those who hurt us.
We believe in Jesus when we shelter the homeless, feed the
hungry, and visit the sick.
We believe in Jesus when we liberate captives and defend
the oppressed.
We believe in Jesus when we welcome strangers.[4]

With our hands and feet, Jesus is tearing down walls and building bridges. To be honest, some of our spanning projects seem completely impractical. Loving our enemy is crazy. And yet Jesus tells us to do precisely that. We protect our property with fences and alarms—even guns. And yet Jesus says that when somebody steals your coat, give him your shirt, too. Forgiving somebody for injuring us just once can seem like impossibly heavy lifting. But Jesus says to forgive seventy times seven times. In other words, the forgiveness well is bottomless.

---

3. Genesis 12:1–3.
4. The baptismal promises in The Book of Common Prayer (pp. 304–5) summarize what a life modeled on Christ looks like.

In Abram's day, every tribe was out only for itself. Conflicts over land and resources were common. The very idea of building a bridge between all these violent, competing tribes must have seemed ludicrous. Nevertheless, that's the dream he pursued. And it's the dream we pursue when we follow Christ. In many respects our world is no less fractious than Abram's. But the hope that moved Abram those many centuries ago still stirs in our hearts today. We will build bridges over even the most forbidding chasms.

Reflection Questions

1. What word, phrase, image, or idea in this chapter stood out to you? What ideas, stories, images, or questions did it suggest to you?

2. Does this chapter make you think of someone you dislike or fear? Someone you judge or resent or harbor a grievance against? Someone you envy or blame or simply can't connect with? Talk about the events that led you to this perspective. Now imagine how Jesus would tell this person's story as his beloved friend.

3. Talk about a time that you were able to mend a strained or broken relationship. What story did you tell about yourself and about the other person before and after the relationship was restored?

4. How has your story about yourself changed as a result of forgiving someone else?

Chapter 15

Claudia, Her Sisters, and the Ascension

Read John 17:20–26.

Claudia, Anna, and Amy made a date to share a pizza. It was the Thanksgiving holiday. As Brené Brown tells us in *Rising Strong*, Claudia was visiting her family in Madison, Wisconsin. Amy—the youngest of these three sisters—had texted Claudia with the pizza invitation. Her idea was to get together without the parents for a little sister time.[1]

As it happened, Amy did not attend Thanksgiving dinner or any holiday event at her parents' home that year. In her late twenties, Amy had struggled with depression and alcoholism since high school. She got sober briefly when she was eighteen, and then spent the next decade in a declining spiral of sobriety and relapse.

Over the years, Amy would show up for some holiday gatherings. When she was drunk, predictable chaos and heartache ensued. On sober visits, her parents lavished attention on her. Their parents' focus on Amy served only to remind Claudia and Anna how Amy's disease had dominated the family dynamic and robbed them of their youth.

This year, Amy's absence infused the family with an aching heaviness. Nobody talked about it. They all just felt the slowly moving

---

1. Brené Brown, *Rising Strong* (New York: Spiegel & Grau, 2015), Kindle loc. 2013ff.

trainwreck that was Amy. And because they were family, they were all going off the rails with her in haunted silence.

Claudia and Anna took leave of their parents to meet Amy for dinner. Claudia later told Brené Brown, "I just thought we could have one meal together. . . . Three sisters sharing a pizza and catching up. Like a normal family."[2]

Amy had texted her address, but as Claudia and Anna got close, they grew increasingly uneasy. Their parents had offered to set Amy up in her own apartment, but Amy had declined. She didn't want their meddling and their control. The surrounding neighborhood was sketchy. Their hearts sank when they rolled up to the actual address. It was a long abandoned store. Plywood covered broken windows. The door was broken.

The reunion did not go well. Anna lit into Amy, and Amy told her to go away. Anna took a cab home. Claudia stayed and listened to Amy talk about how misunderstood she was. Amy pleaded with Claudia to take her back with her to Chicago. Amy could live with her, and Claudia could take care of her little sister. Guilt-stricken, Claudia refused to go along with Amy's plan. After an hour, she got in her car and left.

Brené Brown goes on to recount Claudia's hard, honest work to rumble with her own false narratives and to step toward a healthier place for herself and the ones she loves. And yet as I read Claudia's story, I found myself filtering it through the story of Jesus' Ascension. As a result, the story of Claudia and her sisters became a parable about belonging.

This contemporary parable about three very real sisters reminds us that belonging is more than a feeling that individuals experience. Belonging is a complex interaction between people. We all want to belong. To be more precise, we yearn to belong. Our lives are diminished by isolation and loneliness. Belonging is a need, not a mere lifestyle preference.

We need others to recognize our worth, to acknowledge our dignity, and to accept us as one of their own. Especially in the case of

---

2. Ibid., Kindle loc. 2035–36.

acceptance, we face a spiritual challenge. Whether we like it or not, we long to be accepted for who we really are. And who we really are is always an imperfect mess. Getting real with someone else runs the risk of rejection. Our own fear of being voted off the island can lead us to hide ourselves. Hiding cuts us off from the very acceptance we crave. Belonging takes courage.

It is perhaps not surprising, then, that we can be so focused on being accepted that we miss what should be an obvious point. Genuinely belonging to others means accepting someone else as part of yourself. That we humans struggle to accept difference, much less to embrace it, is old news. Well, actually, that old news keeps making new headlines with some frequency. We threaten to build nation-dividing walls; we argue about who we can refuse service to at our bakeries; and apparently, we are committed to tangling about who goes to what bathroom.

No wonder we end up drawing relatively small circles of genuine belonging. Circles that encompass people whose differences with us don't touch any painfully crucial spots. People essentially like us who will be relatively easy to accept as one of our own. You know. Like family. Like, sisters. Even in our smallest circles, our dysfunctions and fears and limitations and hopes and compulsions and needs and regrets and resentments will make belonging an uneven, painful, beautiful, tangled, poignant mess. At our very best, we will get it right sometimes with some people sort of.

And then the Ascension occurs.[3]

Jesus the risen human being ascends to God's right hand. To heaven. This is all a metaphorical way of relating a mind-bending theological truth. Jesus is fully divine and fully human. The risen Jesus is still fully divine and fully human. When Jesus ascends, he doesn't hit the up button in some elevator. The risen human Jesus is in perfect union with God.

It's not that just one human being cozied up with God. In Jesus, all humanity is in perfect union with God. This continues to be a work in progress. And, as we see in John's Gospel, that's the meaning of

---

3. Acts 1:9–11.

the Ascension. On the night before his crucifixion, Jesus said farewell to his disciples. He washed their feet, shared the Passover meal with them, and taught them about the Holy Spirit. Finally, Jesus steps aside for an intimate conversation with God. He talks about how his work will continue in the lives of his friends after he ascends. He prays, "That they all may be one."[4] All of humanity belongs to God in Jesus. And all of humanity belongs to each other in Jesus.

It's not going to be easy. We really can't get there from here: everybody belonging to everybody. But Jesus can. Jesus did. Jesus will. Jesus told us that he goes ahead of us to prepare a place for us. Not just this person or that person or that other person. For humanity. Together. In union with God. In union with each other. Right where we belong.

Reflection Questions

1. What word, phrase, image, or idea in this chapter stood out to you? What ideas, stories, images, or questions did it suggest to you?
2. Does this chapter make you think of someone you dislike or fear? Someone you judge or resent or harbor a grievance against? Someone you envy or blame or simply can't connect with? Talk about the events that led you to this perspective. Now imagine how Jesus would tell this person's story as his beloved friend.
3. The author writes, "Genuinely belonging to others means accepting someone else as part of yourself." Talk about a time when letting someone else be a part of you was a struggle.
4. Talk about a time when being with another person stretched you and made you someone different.

---

4. John 17:21a.

Chapter 16

Lies and Secrets and Funerals

Read John 20:19–31.

My father died in high summer. The sun had already baked the red Georgia clay into stretches of hard crust across much of the landscape. Tiny black gnats floated drunkenly around eyes and lips and ears. Slow. Persistent. Annoyingly elusive. The Baptist graveside service was scheduled for ten in the morning. Even under the canopy's shade, the sun's heat and the thick, humid air sent beads of sweat rolling down my torso. A black suit in the July heat of South Georgia was a bad idea.

Having flown from St. Louis into Augusta the night before, I drove a rental into Louisville in time to arrive at the burial site about twenty minutes early. Three men in short-sleeved shirts, jeans, and caps stood near the grave. I recognized them as men that my father would hail at Waffle House on my infrequent visits to Louisville. My father would banter with them about fishing while we waited for our take-out order. He never introduced me. I wondered if he actually remembered their names. They looked to me as if they were wondering why this guy was talking to them. When I walked up to them that morning, they studied their shoes as I shook their hands and introduced myself and thanked them for coming. They never told me their names.

We stood there together awkwardly sharing an uncomfortable silence. After what seemed like about a month, the rest of the family pulled up in a couple of limos trailing the hearse. They had gathered beforehand at the funeral home. I must have missed that memo.

Four families connected only by some association with Sam Owensby gathered under the canopy at graveside. Sam's only surviving brother and his wife represented the family of origin. My half-brother and half-sister—along with their spouses and children—shared Sam's first wife as mother and grandmother. I am the only surviving son of wife number two. Wife number three—suffering pitiably of dementia—arrived with her two daughters by her deceased first husband.

Sam was always fond of telling us that we were all one family—brothers and sisters. He made no distinction, so there wasn't one. He was the scion of a great clan. In fact, to hear him tell it, he was widely recognized as a great man. Admired for his hard work and integrity by everybody in that small southern town.

There was tension in the air. Ann, the younger daughter of Sam's third wife, pulled me aside. She said, "Sam passed that letter you sent around to everybody. He wanted us to say how terrible you are. You were very brave to send it. And you were very brave to show up here."

That letter was something a spiritual friend advised me to write. Living with Sam's lie about himself and keeping his secrets had been haunting me. So, I wrote a letter confronting my father with the truth about his control and his abuse and his infidelities and his mendacity.

I showed it to my friend. He read it silently. "Wow. That's an honest letter. Now what do you intend to do with it?"

"I sent it."

"You what?"

"I sent it."

"Oh," he said.

Standing at the grave that day, feeling like a gate crasher, I was wondering just how wise it was to have mailed that letter. Looking back on it from the span of a decade, I would have to say that the jury is still out.

Being in my father's good graces meant giving assent to the lie that he told about himself and keeping his secrets buried. I couldn't do that anymore. Not without doing increasingly severe damage to my own soul and poisoning the relationships I hold dear. And yet, I recognize that my letter was a blunt instrument. Sure, I told the truth. But as one of my old professors used to say, I was doing brain surgery with a buzz saw. Reconciliation is immensely delicate and difficult work. It is God's chief work in Christ. And God has a Church to take up that work; God has disciples—God has you and me. Jesus said it this way. "If you forgive the sins of any, they are forgiven them; if you retain the sins of any, they are retained."[1]

Put simply, forgiveness is the refusal to retaliate for the harm someone else has done to us or to someone we love. When we forgive, we're not sweeping things under the rug. On the contrary, forgiveness begins with holding a guilty party accountable. However, when we forgive, we make the often difficult decision to respond with mercy instead of punishment. Forgiveness can be a unilateral act. Jesus teaches us to forgive even the unrepentant. That's what it means to forgive seventy times seven times. We forgive because of who Jesus is making us, not in response to what someone does or doesn't do.

Reconciliation, by contrast, is always a two-way street. Regaining trust and repairing a fractured relationship requires offending parties to express remorse and to amend their ways. And it involves soul work. Destructive and self-destructive patterns of behavior indicate a deeper spiritual disintegration. Moral misbehavior points toward an abiding injury in the soul. Sinful behavior betrays a shattered soul in need of healing.

I am not excusing wrongdoing by calling attention to the fractured souls that give rise to it. Instead, I am highlighting the deeper work of reconciliation. Jesus doesn't just want to get us off the hook. He wants to make us whole and to make us one. That is the work of reconciliation. It is the work that Jesus gives the Church—gives you and me—to do in the cluttered, unkempt place that is our real lives.

As I look back on my father's funeral, I see things about the man that I simply failed to appreciate when I confronted him with the wounds he had caused. He craved esteem and acceptance. And yet, at the end of his life, that man who claimed to be widely admired had

---

1. John 20:23.

only his quarrelsome family and three acquaintances at his funeral. Caught up at the time in my family drama, I missed how sad and poignant this was. My father had a deep longing to be more than he was. Something profound was missing in his heart and in his sense of his own self-worth. And so he spent a lifetime building and sustaining an elaborate, absurd fiction about himself.

My father had described himself as an indispensable deacon at his Baptist church. And yet, the preacher at that congregation began his sermon this way: "I didn't really know Mr. Sam. . . ." Well, preacher, I guess I didn't really know Mr. Sam either. I saw him only through the pain he had given me. And as a follower of Jesus, I recognize that I can be more than that. In Christ, we can see through our own woundedness to the woundedness of others. Even as we hold them accountable for their moral failings, we can—with Jesus' help—seek to be instruments of healing for their shattered souls.

Reflection Questions

1. What word, phrase, image, or idea in this chapter stood out to you? What ideas, stories, images, or questions did it suggest to you?

2. Does this chapter make you think of someone you dislike or fear? Someone you judge or resent or harbor a grievance against? Someone you envy or blame or simply can't connect with? Talk about the events that led you to this perspective. Now imagine how Jesus would tell this person's story as his beloved friend.

3. Think about someone you are struggling to forgive as flawed and wounded themselves. Does this help you tell a different story about the person? Can you imagine that telling this different story might help you take steps toward forgiveness and reconciliation?

4. Our own wounds and fears can act like lenses through which we see other people. Can you think of a time when your lenses led you to tell a distorted or narrow story about another person? Did learning more about the person change the story you tell?

Part Four

The Sense of an Ending

All such plotting presupposes and requires that an end will bestow upon the whole duration and meaning.
—Frank Kermode, *The Sense of an Ending*

Here, in this life, all symphonies remain unfinished.
—Karl Rahner (in Ronald Rolheiser's *The Holy Longing*)

Chapter 17

Even This

Read Revelation 21:1–6.

My mother, Trudy, used to tell me about a dachshund she once had. When she was feeling low, she would sit on our front stoop. The dog would join her on the top step and lay his head in her lap. From time to time he would look up at her in brown-eyed sympathy. She would say, "He always knew when I was sad. And he would sit with me to make me feel better."

Trudy never sulked or moped about. She loved to laugh and to eat, to cook and to buy gifts for the ones she loved. And yet a continuous stream of tender sadness ran through her heart. During the Second World War, she had endured the allied bombing of her hometown, Linz, Austria. Toward the end of that war, the Nazis confined her to the concentration camp Mauthausen. She had married unwisely, eventually escaping my father's control and abuse after twelve years. Her older son, Joseph, died. And Marie—her only daughter and my little sister—died as well. Sometimes mom would drift back in her memory to earlier days and talk about "my little girl." She was never maudlin or weepy. She seemed to be taken up into a tender nostalgia for what might have been.

This same woman who had suffered so much loss never gave in to despair. Even when we were broke and homeless, she always believed that things were going to look up soon. Her response to my own melt-downs and hissy fits was always the same: "Remember, tomorrow is another day." Paradoxically, my mother knew about hope precisely because she knew about loss and sorrow and pain. Her theology was not sophisticated. Her faith was simple but deep. It could be summed up in this phrase that I borrow from Rob Bell: even this.

God can bring infinite, indescribable beauty, joy, and goodness out of even this. No matter the heartache or the pain, the humiliation or the insane messiness, Jesus redeems it and restores it. He says, "I am making all things new." Even this.[1]

Heaven figured prominently in my mother's experience of hope. And to tell the truth, heaven is a central element of my own sense of hope. My first theological lesson came from my mother.

My little sister, Marie, died when I was three. Her life was fleeting, and I have no memories of her. Instead, I remember experiencing her absence. My mother comforted me—and no doubt comforted herself—by telling me that Marie was in heaven. One day, we would see her again. Even this. Jesus will redeem even this. The loss of a child. The shattered heart of a mother. A child's confusion and sorrow. Even this.

As a child, I thought of heaven as a place that we go after we die. Like many people then and now, I pictured a paradise to which my sister's soul had flown. After all, my night prayer was the one that many of my contemporaries would likely recognize:

Now I lay me down to sleep. I pray the Lord my soul to keep.
And if I die before I wake, I pray the Lord my soul to take.

Some people start thinking about heaven as they face their own mortality. They understandably wonder what will happen to them after they die. By contrast, my thinking about heaven began with my sister's death. My question—even as a child—was not what would happen to me when I died. Instead, I wondered what happened to one I loved but could see no longer.

My thoughts about heaven are never merely ideas. There is a yearning for heaven in my soul: a longing for peace and healing for those who have gone ahead of me to a distant shore; a desire that the

---

1. Revelation 21:5.

circle be unbroken for all eternity. And now I realize that a yearning for God's perpetual presence in our midst lies at the very heart of my thoughts. For it is in Christ that all will be well. All will be made whole.

The author of Revelation teaches us that what I have been calling heaven is shorthand for something far more thrilling and mind-blowing than a place that good souls inhabit. God will come to dwell in our midst. God's presence will transform our bruised and battered world into a new heaven and a new earth. In Jesus God heals the physical, moral, and emotional injuries of the world. Heaven is this very place, but in a future appointed by God and transformed by God's perfect, abiding presence. This place. In all its sorrows and selfishness, in all its deprivation and oppression, in all its indifference and violence, this place will be transformed. Made new. Even this. God "will wipe every tear from their eyes. Death will be no more; mourning and crying and pain will be no more, for the first things have passed away."[2]

Jesus' resurrection is the first wave in God's restoration of the fractured creation. Jesus is the beginning of the new creation. And by following Jesus we are taken up in the wake of the new creation. When each of us crosses over to the other shore, we will look back at the lives we lived in this time and space and say, "Why, heaven was already happening. Even there." Our most joyful moments will look to us as anticipations of the infinite joy we will then know in immortal flesh. The heartaches and suffering and even our moral failures will seem to us from heaven's perspective to be the wounds that were already being healed. As professor, Catholic priest, and my friend, Tom, once told me, "I don't know what heaven's plumbing looks like, but I believe." Jesus is making all things new. Even this.

Two decades have passed since my mother died. I sometimes ache from missing her. I am comforted by images of her spiritual body strolling through alpine meadows strewn with spring flowers. Laughing and running and playing with her little girl, Marie, and our brother, Joseph. All of them trailed by a dachshund whose stubby legs can barely keep pace. In their midst stands the risen Jesus, in whom and by whom and

---

2. Revelation 21:4.

through whom they all inhabit a new heaven and a new earth. God will not discard this creation. Neither will God destroy it. In Jesus, God is even now making all things new. Even this.

Reflection Questions

1. What word, phrase, image, or idea in this chapter stood out to you? What ideas, stories, images, or questions did it suggest to you?

2. The chapters in this final section invite readers to imagine the ending that bestows meaning on the story of their lives. How has this chapter helped you to think about that ending? Recall an episode of your life that you still struggle to understand or accept. Does this chapter's portrayal of eternal life offer a new way to talk about that episode?

3. In this chapter the author says that heaven is not a place we go after we die. Instead, God renews the creation by dwelling in its midst for eternity. Discuss this idea. How does this shape the story you tell about yourself and others?

4. Do you have hope for your future? For the future of those you love? Upon what do you place that hope?

Chapter 18

A Happier Place

Read Luke 4:21–30.

My fourth-grade teacher took a dim view of me. At least, that's how it seemed at the time. Take, for instance, the playground incident I was involved in.

It was a sunny late spring morning. The whole class was playing softball. I was up to bat, waiting for the pitch, when a hard blow to the back of my leg knocked me to the ground. A boy named Steve had hit me with a bat before anybody realized what was happening. For the record, Steve and I had run-ins from time to time. We also played together fairly regularly. Boys. Right? And on this occasion I had probably trash-talked him about something, but I hadn't laid a hand on him.

Our teacher ran up as I lay on the ground fighting back tears with only minimal success. Her precise words escape me now, but she was scolding me and saying something about knowing what I was like. She imposed some punishment on me and began comforting Steve as if I had stuck a hot poker in his eye. I do remember a girl named Julie telling our teacher, "But he didn't do anything. Steve just snuck up on him and hit him for no reason." What Julie said didn't matter. I got punished and I got the message. My teacher was almost as glad as I was to soon be moving on to fifth grade and out of her class. Hope came to me in the form of a rapidly approaching summer break and a new teacher in the fall. I would soon escape to a happier place.

No matter how sweet and good this life can be, millions of people find comfort and hope in the belief that when this life is over we will be in a happier place. In a paradise where the cares, sorrows, and trials of this world are forever in the past. If you poll a sample of these people about what heaven looks like, you're likely to hear a variety of descriptions. For instance, somebody once told me that paradise would be spending every day duck hunting. I have to tell you, that sounded like a pretty crummy deal for the ducks to me. But this duck hunter's portrait of the afterlife has one thing in common with many of the images I've heard from other people. Heaven is the place where you get to do the stuff you love to do forever.

They figure a Savior's role is to get you into your own eternal holodeck. For those unfamiliar with Star Trek, the holodeck is a compartment in the starship *Enterprise* where crew members can enter and call up any perfect holographic world they want: Wild West, medieval castle, deer stand, you name it. You just tell the computer and it will put you in the scenario of your choice, complete with sights, smells, sounds, tastes, and even a supporting cast of characters. Some think of paradise like a celestial holodeck. It's a setting filled with everything that pleases you, and you don't have to share it with anybody you don't want in there. Pretty great, huh? Only, that's not what Jesus offers.

Jesus did not come to transport each of us to our own private paradise. For that matter, he didn't come to make a space for us to gather with all our favorite people undisturbed by jerks, lowlifes, deadbeats, and creeps. On the contrary, Jesus came to prepare us to sit together at one table at a great feast. Eternal life is neither luxurious solitary play nor a ceaseless romp with your own select in-group. The Great Heavenly Banquet has a vast guest list over which we have no control.

Paradoxically, Jesus aims to create an intimacy at this vast party that is nearer and gentler than anything we have yet experienced. It's as if we will sit directly across the table from each person. Hearing and seeing, being heard and being seen. Without pretense. Without judgment. In perfect empathy and tender acceptance for the imperfect, messy gifts we are to one another. Christ himself is drawing us together and opening us up to each other.

As it turns out, the greatest obstacle to entering the Kingdom of God is our capacity to label others as a jerk, lowlife, deadbeat, or creep where Jesus sees each as a child of God. The Kingdom of God is where loving your neighbor as yourself—loving your neighbor as if you shared an inseparable circulatory system—becomes an eternal reality. Getting us ready for the Kingdom is what Jesus does. That's what it means to say that Jesus is our Savior. Because let's just face it, there are plenty of people we flinch at seeing on the guest list of the heavenly party. Or at the very least, we would like to see them assigned to a different table. Maybe even an entirely separate dining hall. We know we're supposed to love our neighbor. And we're really fine with that. So long as we get to choose our neighbors and nobody irritating, offensive, threatening, or distasteful is forced on us.

Here is where Jesus's teaching in the synagogue at Nazareth took such a bad turn. He had just proclaimed himself to be the Savior. He had come to bring good news to the poor, free the captive, give relief to the oppressed, restore sight to the blind, and make the lame walk. So far so good. Then he sticks his foot in it. God's salvation makes neighbors of people you've considered your inferiors and even your enemies. And he gives examples that are familiar to them: Through the prophet Elijah, God fed the widow of Zarephath throughout a years-long drought and even raised her son from the dead. Only, she wasn't an Israelite. Through the prophet Elisha, God healed Naaman of leprosy. Naaman wasn't just a Syrian. He was a commander. Of an opposing army.

The congregation in Nazareth erupted. Jesus suggesting that salvation included loving a foreign beggar and a military enemy as blood of their own blood? Maybe some in the congregation thought and felt that the widow, and certainly Naaman, didn't act like neighbors. They had different values and competing goals. And they may even drain the resources of and pose a threat to the Israelites. But Jesus didn't mean that we should assess who passes a set of eligibility requirements for being considered a neighbor. Jesus taught that we must act like neighbors first, and that a neighbor is someone who shows compassion (Luke 10:36–37). In other words, Jesus calls his followers to be neighbors to everyone we meet. A compassionate heart treats others as neighbors because that is who we are in Christ, not because someone merits our respect and understanding by what they have achieved or how they act or what they think.

As it turns out, this is a happier place. The happiest place. This is the Kingdom of God, the kingdom where healing, restoring, reconciling love reigns supreme. Love like this is very difficult. In fact, for us, it's impossible. And that is why we need a savior.

Reflection Questions

1. What word, phrase, image, or idea in this chapter stood out to you? What ideas, stories, images, or questions did it suggest to you?

2. The chapters in this final section invite readers to imagine the ending that bestows meaning on the story of their lives. How has this chapter helped you to think about that ending? Recall an episode of your life that you still struggle to understand or accept. Does this chapter's portrayal of eternal life offer a new way to talk about that episode?

3. In this chapter the author portrays the ending of our stories using the image of the Great Heavenly Banquet. We will sit across from people with whom we have had conflict or from whom we have recoiled or against whom we have had resentments. Discuss your response to this idea. How would God get you ready for such a Banquet?

4. Do you have hope for your future? For the future of those you love? Given what you have read in this chapter, upon what do you place that hope?

Chapter 19

Dirty Laundry

R*ead Hebrews 11:1–3, 8–16.*

In Gail Godwin's novel *Father Melancholy's Daughter*, a character named Katharine shares a lesson she learned while on retreat at a monastery.[1] It's a lesson that Jesus and the writer of Hebrews conveyed long ago.

A retreat among the brothers can involve full participation in the rhythms of monastic life. Benedict famously summarized the pattern of their community with the phrase *"ora et labora"*: pray and work. At set times each day, the monks pray together and work together. Katharine gathered with the community for prayer, and she accepted a work assignment. Between 9:00 a.m. and 1:00 p.m., she and one of the monks served in the laundry room.

The washing machine was an ancient, outdated model. It had one of those wringers for the clothes. On their first day together, the monk steadily put each item of clothing through the wringer. Katharine took each item and hung it out to dry in the sun. As the morning stretched toward the afternoon, Katharine realized that there were still heaps and heaps of dirty clothes. She began grabbing the clothes from the monk and rushing to the clothes line. Finally, he asked her why she was in such a frantic hurry. Here's their exchange:

---

1. Gail Godwin, *Father Melancholy's Daughter* (New York: Perennial, 1991).

"We're never going to finish all these baskets by one," she said, almost in tears.

"We don't have to," he told her. "Someone else will finish them. All that is required of us is that we work, steadily and for the glory of God, from nine until one, at our appointed task every day."[2]

The wise monk, the writer of Hebrews, and Jesus himself are telling us an essential truth about following Jesus. God has a mission. In Jesus, God is restoring and healing this shattered, wounded creation. Over time. Over lots and lots of time. Waiting and watching and persevering come with the territory.

Jesus engaged God's mission with his own earthly hands and feet throughout Judea. He befriended outcasts, cleansed lepers, and liberated people from their demons. Jesus fed multitudes, brought the dead back to life, and faced down power figures who exploited the weak, the powerless, and the needy. Jesus continues the very same work with earthly hands and feet—our hands and feet. The Church is the people of God saturated by the Holy Spirit at Baptism. We are the very hands and feet of Jesus.

Jesus did not come to provide an escape hatch from here to paradise. Leaving the creation behind isn't in God's game plan. Everything that is came to be from the depths of God's love. God doesn't abandon, much less destroy, the beloved when things get rough. God makes things right again. Think about how Jesus taught us to pray: thy Kingdom come. In the Revelation to John, we read that the New Jerusalem will descend. God will dwell forever in our midst, and God's presence renews the heavens and the earth. As we say in our creeds, Jesus will come again to reign.

God created the world to be a place of justice and mercy, compassion and peace. Suffering and hunger, prejudice and violence, terror and sorrow are hideous distortions of God's beautiful handiwork. And through the hands of Jesus—through your hands and my

---

2. Ibid., p. 65.

hands—God is restoring the whole creation to its intended grace and harmony. Eventually.

In a world tossed by war and crime, rent by deprivation and oppression, degraded by greed and indifference, we can grow discouraged. Our courage and kindness and generosity can seem pitiably inadequate to enormous tasks like bringing lasting peace, eradicating hunger, and restoring trust among races. And yet, Jesus tells us to do the good that we can do. Stay alert and keep our lamps burning. God is already at work in ways that we cannot fully discern. God is not finished, but God is surely at work. At work in the things great and small that we do each day to engage God's mission. Like Abraham, we may catch a glimpse of the promised completion. As the writer of Hebrews says about many of our forerunners in the faith, "All of these died in faith without having received the promises, but from a distance they saw and greeted them."[3]

I suppose you might say that God assigns each of us to some version of the laundry room. There are piles and piles of dirty clothes to wash and dry. We won't finish them all in the time God has allotted. But this does not mean that our work has been pointless or that it has come to nothing. We are doing our part, and that is all that God is asking. When our appointed time comes to an end and we pass from life to eternal life, others will come and take up their part in completing the laundry.

Faith becomes real when we put our hands to the wringer and pin clothes to the line. Our hope lies in the belief that we do not do this on our own. This is, after all, God's laundry. And God is doing it through us. And once God starts something, God brings is to completion. Eventually.

Reflection Questions

1. What word, phrase, image, or idea in this chapter stood out to you? What ideas, stories, images, or questions did it suggest to you?

---

3. Hebrews 11:13.

2. The chapters in this final section invite readers to imagine the ending that bestows meaning on the story of their lives. How has this chapter helped you to think about that ending? Recall an episode of your life that you still struggle to understand or accept. Does this chapter's portrayal of eternal life offer a new way to talk about that episode?

3. Talk about a time that you have felt overwhelmed by or discouraged by the persistence and the enormity of your family's struggles or the world's problems? What encouraged you to take the next step and to persevere?

4. Do you have hope for your future? For the future of those you love? Given what you have read in this chapter, upon what do you place that hope?

Chapter 20

Until Morning

Read Luke 7:11–17.

Much of my childhood and all of my teen years were spent living in my grandparents' home with my mother. They had all immigrated to the United States from Austria in the early 1950s. First my mom came over, followed a couple of years later by her parents.

They all spoke in English to me but in German with each other. Well, actually, my grandparents frequently spoke a kind of mixed English and German to me. My guess is that they always thought in German and then struggled to translate using their limited vocabulary and shaky grammar. For instance, we didn't usually say, "Good night." Sometimes we would say, "Gute Nacht!" or "Schlaf gut!" "Good night" and "sleep well" in German. But more frequently, we would say, "Bis Morgen!" Until morning! Maybe you say, "See you in the morning."

I'm fond of this phrase. It connotes that we will see each other again after a brief separation. Our connection to each other is not severed even though we are absent from each other's sight. My grandparents and my mother died years ago. My last book, *Gospel Memories*, is dedicated to them: "To Trudy, Joseph, and Marie . . . Bis Morgen!" Joseph and Marie were my grandparents; my older brother and my younger sister also bore these same names. All died years ago. The dedication in *Gospel Memories* conveys my sense that—even though they are obscured from my sight—my mother, my grandparents, and my siblings remain deeply connected to me. "Bis Morgen" expresses my hope that I will see them by a morning light that I have only partially glimpsed. The morning of the New Heaven and the New Earth. A morning that never fades into night. I believe in the resurrection. And what I believe about the resurrection shapes how I lead this life.

Jesus teaches about life and death.

On his way across the countryside, Jesus comes to a little town called Nain. Just as he gets to the city gate, he runs into a funeral procession. A widow's only son has died, and they are carrying his corpse beyond the city walls for burial. Jesus responds with compassion. He understands the widow's grief because he's been there. His own mother has been a widow since they buried his earthly father, Joseph. He also understands the widow's plight. In that culture, a woman without a male benefactor—like a husband or a son—would be destitute. That is perhaps one reason why his mother, Mary, accompanied Jesus on his ministry.

Jesus' empathy is no mere feeling. It is the power of divine love: the power to feed a multitude with a few loaves and to calm stormy seas; the power to heal lepers, to bring sight to the blind, and to make the lame walk; the power to bring life out of death. And that is precisely what Jesus did. With a few words, Jesus restored the dead man to life.

This is quite a miracle. But it is only a resuscitation. Jesus brought the man back to an earthly life in which he would once again know sorrow, pain, and death. When Jesus emerged from the tomb, his was a life that had passed through death. He didn't just come back from the dead. He is on the other side of death once and for all. Jesus came to give us that kind of life.

The kind of life we can give ourselves is no doubt good. We can have family and friends, material comforts and pleasant entertainments. We can have rewarding careers, undertake fascinating studies, discover cures for dreadful diseases, and create great pieces of art. We can sing together and dance together and eat crawfish together. But we can't bring ourselves back from the dead. And we cannot make a life that is impervious to heartbreak, disappointment, aging, sickness, and plain bad luck.

Only Jesus can give us that kind of life. Only Jesus brings resurrection. And to use a phrase I attribute to the late Robert Farrar Capon, the story of the widow's son teaches us that resurrection is only for the dead. The dead have no pretense to self-help and self-improvement. They are radically dependent upon someone beyond themselves to give them life. And by raising the widow's son from the dead, Jesus is telling us that his Way is a way of radical dependence upon God.

The new life in Christ begins even now as we surrender ourselves in humility to the power of divine compassion. Neither our moral rectitude nor our rigorous piety nor our well-crafted theologies will give us life eternal. Only Jesus does that. And when we trust Jesus to give us life eternal, heaven begins to infiltrate earth. We can begin to know a peace that surpasses anything that our achievements or possessions could possibly convey. And we're able to nurture people and be nurtured by them in surprising and enduring ways. Charleen Klister is a person like that.

Charleen was my sophomore English teacher at St. Pius X Catholic High School. She taught me not only to write, but how to pursue a dream: the dream of doing good by writing. She once heard me say something like, "I'll never be president of the United States." Charleen must have seen how I had come to believe that a person with my background and my limitations could never do anything of great worth. Never make a difference. She gently stopped me and asked, "Why not? Why couldn't you be president? Of course you could." This was not some self-esteem pep talk. She was calling me on my psychological baggage. Challenging me to take risks and to quit giving myself excuses for passing up opportunities to make the world a better place.

A few days before she died, Charlene contacted me. We spoke for a few minutes on the phone. She had recently retired from St. Pius, and she was in hospice. She sounded like the old Charleen I remembered. Her voice was a bit thinner and weaker, but as clear and gracious as ever. She wanted to tell me that I am loved. Above all, she wanted me to know that. Her love for me—and my love for her—has stretched over these many years and many miles to keep us connected. I realized that her love for me is what changed my life. It was Jesus' love that flowed through her. And that love flows through me back to her. She shared with me that, as her earthly life was unwinding, God was surrounding her with peace and beauty from the most surprising and wonderful places and people. She was completely at peace with passing from life to life.

At the end of our conversation, she said, "Good night."

It was still afternoon, and I took this to mean, "Until we meet again on that far shore."

I said, "Bis Morgen."

"Yes," she said, "Until morning."

Reflection Questions

1. What word, phrase, image, or idea in this chapter stood out to you? What ideas, stories, images, or questions did it suggest to you?

2. The chapters in this final section invite readers to imagine the ending that bestows meaning on the story of their lives. How has this chapter helped you to think about that ending? Recall an episode of your life that you still struggle to understand or accept. Does this chapter's portrayal of eternal life offer a new way to talk about that episode?

3. Have you said a final earthly good-bye to someone you love? How did that influence your sense of your own time in this life? Do you have a sense of anticipation about life after life? How does it shape the story you tell about yourself and others now?

4. Do you have hope for your future? For the future of those you love? Given what you have read in this chapter, upon what do you place that hope?

APPENDIX A
SCRIPTURE INDEX

Genesis 15:1–12, 17–18 (Lent 2C)	59, 100
Matthew 3:13–17 (Epiphany 1A)	11, 92
Matthew 3:1–12 (Advent 2A)	47, 97
Luke 4:21–30 (Epiphany 4C)	77, 103
Luke 7:11–17 (Proper 5C)	85, 105
Luke 7:36–8:3 (Proper 6C)	51, 98
Luke 10:25–37 (Proper 10C)	55, 99
Luke 17:5–10 (Proper 22C)	3, 91
Luke 17:11–19 (Proper 23C)	25, 94
Luke 19:1–10 (Proper 26C)	37, 96
Luke 21:5–19 (Proper 28C)	15, 92
Luke 23:33–43 (Proper 29C)	19, 93
John 14:23–29 (Easter 6C)	7, 92
John 17:20–26 (Easter 7C)	63, 101
John 20:19–31 (Easter 2A, 2B, 2C)	67, 102
John 21:1–19 (Easter 3C)	29, 94
Hebrews 11:1–3 (Proper 14C)	81, 104
Hebrews 12:18–29 (Proper 16C)	41, 97
Revelation 21:1–6 (Easter 5C)	73, 103

APPENDIX B
SCRIPTURE STORIES

Chapter 1: All They're Going to Get Is You

Luke 17:5–10

The apostles said to the Lord, "Increase our faith!" The Lord replied, "If you had faith the size of a mustard seed, you could say to this mulberry tree, 'Be uprooted and planted in the sea,' and it would obey you.

"Who among you would say to your slave who has just come in from plowing or tending sheep in the field, 'Come here at once and take your place at the table'? Would you not rather say to him, 'Prepare supper for me, put on your apron and serve me while I eat and drink; later you may eat and drink'? Do you thank the slave for doing what was commanded? So you also, when you have done all that you were ordered to do, say, 'We are worthless slaves; we have done only what we ought to have done!'"

Chapter 2: Keeping Our Word

John 14:23–29

Jesus answered him, "Those who love me will keep my word, and my Father will love them, and we will come to them and make our home with them. Whoever does not love me does not keep my words; and the word that you hear is not mine, but is from the Father who sent me.

"I have said these things to you while I am still with you. But the Advocate, the Holy Spirit, whom the Father will send in my name, will teach you everything, and remind you of all that I have said to you.

Peace I leave with you; my peace I give to you. I do not give to you as the world gives. Do not let your hearts be troubled, and do not let them be afraid. You heard me say to you, 'I am going away, and I am coming to you.' If you loved me, you would rejoice that I am going to the Father, because the Father is greater than I. And now I have told you this before it occurs, so that when it does occur, you may believe."

Chapter 3: In Our Very Bones

Matthew 3:13–17

Then Jesus came from Galilee to John at the Jordan, to be baptized by him. John would have prevented him, saying, "I need to be baptized by you, and do you come to me?" But Jesus answered him, "Let it be so now; for it is proper for us in this way to fulfill all righteousness." Then he consented. And when Jesus had been baptized, just as he came up from the water, suddenly the heavens were opened to him and he saw the Spirit of God descending like a dove and alighting on him. And a voice from heaven said, "This is my Son, the Beloved, with whom I am well pleased."

Chapter 4: Jesus and Nietzsche Walk into a Bar

Luke 21:5–19

When some were speaking about the temple, how it was adorned with beautiful stones and gifts dedicated to God, he said, "As for these things that you see, the days will come when not one stone will be left upon another; all will be thrown down."

They asked him, "Teacher, when will this be, and what will be the sign that this is about to take place?" And he said, "Beware that you are not led astray; for many will come in my name and say, 'I am he!' and, 'The time is near!' Do not go after them.

"When you hear of wars and insurrections, do not be terrified; for these things must take place first, but the end will not follow immediately." Then he said to them, "Nation will rise against nation, and kingdom against kingdom; there will be great earthquakes, and in various places famines and plagues; and there will be dreadful portents and great signs from heaven.

"But before all this occurs, they will arrest you and persecute you; they will hand you over to synagogues and prisons, and you will be brought before kings and governors because of my name. This will give you an opportunity to testify. So make up your minds not to prepare your defense in advance; for I will give you words and a wisdom that none of your opponents will be able to withstand or contradict. You will be betrayed even by parents and brothers, by relatives and friends; and they will put some of you to death. You will be hated by all because of my name. But not a hair of your head will perish. By your endurance you will gain your souls.

Chapter 5: Jesus, Clark Kent, and Quentin Tarantino

Luke 23:33–43

When they came to the place that is called The Skull, they crucified Jesus there with the criminals, one on his right and one on his left. Then Jesus said, "Father, forgive them; for they do not know what they are doing." And they cast lots to divide his clothing. And the people stood by, watching; but the leaders scoffed at him, saying, "He saved others; let him save himself if he is the Messiah of God, his chosen one!" The soldiers also mocked him, coming up and offering him sour wine, and saying, "If you are the King of the Jews, save yourself!" There was also an inscription over him, "This is the King of the Jews."

One of the criminals who were hanged there kept deriding him and saying, "Are you not the Messiah? Save yourself and us!" But the other rebuked him, saying, "Do you not fear God, since you are under the same sentence of condemnation? And we indeed have been condemned justly, for we are getting what we deserve for our deeds, but this man has done nothing wrong." Then he said, "Jesus, remember me when you come into your kingdom." He replied, "Truly I tell you, today you will be with me in Paradise."

Chapter 6: Hearing Grace

Luke 17:11–19

On the way to Jerusalem Jesus was going through the region between Samaria and Galilee. As he entered a village, ten lepers approached him. Keeping their distance, they called out, saying, "Jesus, Master, have mercy on us!" When he saw them, he said to them, "Go and show yourselves to the priests." And as they went, they were made clean. Then one of them, when he saw that he was healed, turned back, praising God with a loud voice. He prostrated himself at Jesus' feet and thanked him. And he was a Samaritan. Then Jesus asked, "Were not ten made clean? But the other nine, where are they? Was none of them found to return and give praise to God except this foreigner?" Then he said to him, "Get up and go on your way; your faith has made you well."

Chapter 7: Forgiving Yourself

John 21:1–19

After these things Jesus showed himself again to the disciples by the Sea of Tiberias; and he showed himself in this way. Gathered there together were Simon Peter, Thomas called the Twin, Nathanael of Cana in Galilee, the sons of Zebedee, and two others of his disciples. Simon Peter said to them, "I am going fishing." They said to him, "We will go with you." They went out and got into the boat, but that night they caught nothing.

Just after daybreak, Jesus stood on the beach; but the disciples did not know that it was Jesus. Jesus said to them, "Children, you have no fish, have you?" They answered him, "No." He said to them, "Cast the net to the right side of the boat, and you will find some." So they cast it, and now they were not able to haul it in because there were so many fish. That disciple whom Jesus loved said to Peter, "It is the Lord!" When Simon Peter heard that it was the Lord, he put on some clothes, for he was naked, and jumped into the sea. But the other disciples came in the boat, dragging the net full of fish, for they were not far from the land, only about a hundred yards off.

When they had gone ashore, they saw a charcoal fire there, with fish on it, and bread. Jesus said to them, "Bring some of the fish that you have just caught." So Simon Peter went aboard and hauled the net ashore, full of large fish, a hundred fifty-three of them; and though there were so many, the net was not torn. Jesus said to them, "Come and have breakfast." Now none of the disciples dared to ask him, "Who are you?" because they knew it was the Lord. Jesus came and took the bread and gave it to them, and did the same with the fish. This was now the third time that Jesus appeared to the disciples after he was raised from the dead.

When they had finished breakfast, Jesus said to Simon Peter, "Simon son of John, do you love me more than these?" He said to him, "Yes, Lord; you know that I love you." Jesus said to him, "Feed my lambs." A second time he said to him, "Simon son of John, do you love me?" He said to him, "Yes, Lord; you know that I love you." Jesus said to him, "Tend my sheep." He said to him the third time, "Simon son of John, do you love me?" Peter felt hurt because he said to him the third time, "Do you love me?" And he said to him, "Lord, you know everything; you know that I love you." Jesus said to him, "Feed my sheep. Very truly, I tell you, when you were younger, you used to fasten your own belt and to go wherever you wished. But when you grow old, you will stretch out your hands, and someone else will fasten a belt around you and take you where you do not wish to go." (He said this to indicate the kind of death by which he would glorify God.) After this he said to him, "Follow me."

Chapter 8: Boiled Shrimp and Broken Toys

Luke 13:1–9

At that very time there were some present who told him about the Galileans whose blood Pilate had mingled with their sacrifices. He asked them, "Do you think that because these Galileans suffered in this way they were worse sinners than all other Galileans? No, I tell you; but unless you repent, you will all perish as they did. Or those eighteen who were killed when the tower of Siloam fell on them—do you think that they were worse offenders than all the others living in Jerusalem? No, I tell you; but unless you repent, you will all perish just as they did."

Then he told this parable: "A man had a fig tree planted in his vineyard; and he came looking for fruit on it and found none. So he said to the gardener, 'See here! For three years I have come looking for fruit on this fig tree, and still I find none. Cut it down! Why should it be wasting the soil?' He replied, 'Sir, let it alone for one more year, until I dig around it and put manure on it. If it bears fruit next year, well and good; but if not, you can cut it down.'"

Chapter 9: Restoring Our Sanity

Luke 19:1–10

He entered Jericho and was passing through it. A man was there named Zacchaeus; he was a chief tax collector and was rich. He was trying to see who Jesus was, but on account of the crowd he could not, because he was short in stature. So he ran ahead and climbed a sycamore tree to see him, because he was going to pass that way. When Jesus came to the place, he looked up and said to him, "Zacchaeus, hurry and come down; for I must stay at your house today." So he hurried down and was happy to welcome him. All who saw it began to grumble and said, "He has gone to be the guest of one who is a sinner." Zacchaeus stood there and said to the Lord, "Look, half of my possessions, Lord, I will give to the poor; and if I have defrauded anyone of anything, I will pay back four times as much." Then Jesus said to him, "Today salvation has come to this house, because he too is a son of Abraham. For the Son of Man came to seek out and to save the lost."

Chapter 10: Stretching Each Other

Hebrews 12:18–29

You have not come to something that can be touched, a blazing fire, and darkness, and gloom, and a tempest, and the sound of a trumpet, and a voice whose words made the hearers beg that not another word be spoken to them. (For they could not endure the order that was given, "If even an animal touches the mountain, it shall be stoned to death." Indeed, so terrifying was the sight that Moses said, "I tremble with fear.") But you have come to Mount Zion and to the city of the living God, the heavenly Jerusalem, and to innumerable angels in festal gathering, and to the assembly of the firstborn who are enrolled in heaven, and to God the judge of all, and to the spirits of the righteous made perfect, and to Jesus, the mediator of a new covenant, and to the sprinkled blood that speaks a better word than the blood of Abel.

See that you do not refuse the one who is speaking; for if they did not escape when they refused the one who warned them on earth, how much less will we escape if we reject the one who warns from heaven! At that time his voice shook the earth; but now he has promised, "Yet once more I will shake not only the earth but also the heaven." This phrase, "Yet once more," indicates the removal of what is shaken— that is, created things—so that what cannot be shaken may remain. Therefore, since we are receiving a kingdom that cannot be shaken, let us give thanks, by which we offer to God an acceptable worship with reverence and awe; for indeed our God is a consuming fire.

Chapter 11: Being Normal Almost Killed Me

Matthew 3:1–12

In those days John the Baptist appeared in the wilderness of Judea, proclaiming, "Repent, for the kingdom of heaven has come near." This is the one of whom the prophet Isaiah spoke when he said,

"The voice of one crying out in the wilderness:
  'Prepare the way of the Lord,
    make his paths straight.'"

Now John wore clothing of camel's hair with a leather belt around his waist, and his food was locusts and wild honey. Then the people of Jerusalem and all Judea were going out to him, and all the region along the Jordan, and they were baptized by him in the river Jordan, confessing their sins.

But when he saw many Pharisees and Sadducees coming for baptism, he said to them, "You brood of vipers! Who warned you to flee from the wrath to come? Bear fruit worthy of repentance. Do not presume to say to yourselves, 'We have Abraham as our ancestor'; for I tell you, God is able from these stones to raise up children to Abraham. Even now the ax is lying at the root of the trees; every tree therefore that does not bear good fruit is cut down and thrown into the fire.

"I baptize you with water for repentance, but one who is more powerful than I is coming after me; I am not worthy to carry his sandals. He will baptize you with the Holy Spirit and fire. His winnowing fork is in his hand, and he will clear his threshing floor and will gather his wheat into the granary; but the chaff he will burn with unquenchable fire."

Chapter 12: Ugly Love

Luke 7:36–8:3

One of the Pharisees asked Jesus to eat with him, and he went into the Pharisee's house and took his place at the table. And a woman in the city, who was a sinner, having learned that he was eating in the Pharisee's house, brought an alabaster jar of ointment. She stood behind him at his feet, weeping, and began to bathe his feet with her tears and to dry them with her hair. Then she continued kissing his feet and anointing them with the ointment. Now when the Pharisee who had invited him saw it, he said to himself, "If this man were a prophet, he would have known who and what kind of woman this is who is touching him—that she is a sinner." Jesus spoke up and said to him, "Simon, I have something to say to you." "Teacher," he replied, "Speak." "A certain creditor had two debtors; one owed five hundred denarii, and the other fifty. When they could not pay, he canceled the debts for both of them. Now which of them will love him more?" Simon answered, "I suppose the one for whom he canceled the greater debt." And Jesus said to him, "You have judged rightly." Then turning toward the woman, he said to Simon, "Do you see this woman? I entered your house; you gave me no water for my feet, but she has bathed my feet with her tears and dried them with her hair. You gave me no kiss, but from the time I came in she has not stopped kissing my feet. You did not anoint my head with oil, but she has anointed my feet with ointment. Therefore, I tell you, her sins, which were many, have been forgiven; hence she has shown great love. But the one to whom little is forgiven, loves little." Then he said to her, "Your sins are forgiven." But those who were at the table with him began to say among themselves, "Who is this who even forgives sins?" And he said to the woman, "Your faith has saved you; go in peace."

Soon afterwards he went on through cities and villages, proclaiming and bringing the good news of the kingdom of God. The twelve were with him, as well as some women who had been cured of evil spirits and infirmities: Mary, called Magdalene, from whom seven demons had gone out, and Joanna, the wife of Herod's steward Chuza, and Susanna, and many others, who provided for them out of their resources.

Chapter 13: Not Those People

Luke 10:25–37

Just then a lawyer stood up to test Jesus. "Teacher," he said, "what must I do to inherit eternal life?" He said to him, "What is written in the law? What do you read there?" He answered, "You shall love the Lord your God with all your heart, and with all your soul, and with all your strength, and with all your mind; and your neighbor as yourself." And he said to him, "You have given the right answer; do this, and you will live."

But wanting to justify himself, he asked Jesus, "And who is my neighbor?" Jesus replied, "A man was going down from Jerusalem to Jericho, and fell into the hands of robbers, who stripped him, beat him, and went away, leaving him half dead. Now by chance a priest was going down that road; and when he saw him, he passed by on the other side. So likewise a Levite, when he came to the place and saw him, passed by on the other side. But a Samaritan while traveling came near him; and when he saw him, he was moved with pity. He went to him and bandaged his wounds, having poured oil and wine on them. Then he put him on his own animal, brought him to an inn, and took care of him. The next day he took out two denarii, gave them to the innkeeper, and said, 'Take care of him; and when I come back, I will repay you whatever more you spend.' Which of these three, do you think, was a neighbor to the man who fell into the hands of the robbers?" He said, "The one who showed him mercy." Jesus said to him, "Go and do likewise."

Chapter 14: Walls and Bridges

Genesis 15:1–12, 17–18

After these things the word of the LORD came to Abram in a vision, "Do not be afraid, Abram, I am your shield; your reward shall be very great." But Abram said, "O Lord GOD, what will you give me, for I continue childless, and the heir of my house is Eliezer of Damascus?" And Abram said, "You have given me no offspring, and so a slave born in my house is to be my heir." But the word of the LORD came to him, "This man shall not be your heir; no one but your very own issue shall be your heir." He brought him outside and said, "Look toward heaven and count the stars, if you are able to count them." Then he said to him, "So shall your descendants be." And he believed the LORD; and the LORD reckoned it to him as righteousness.

Then he said to him, "I am the LORD who brought you from Ur of the Chaldeans, to give you this land to possess." But he said, "O Lord GOD, how am I to know that I shall possess it?" He said to him, "Bring me a heifer three years old, a female goat three years old, a ram three years old, a turtledove, and a young pigeon." He brought him all these and cut them in two, laying each half over against the other; but he did not cut the birds in two. And when birds of prey came down on the carcasses, Abram drove them away.

As the sun was going down, a deep sleep fell upon Abram, and a deep and terrifying darkness descended upon him. . . .

When the sun had gone down and it was dark, a smoking fire pot and a flaming torch passed between these pieces. On that day the LORD made a covenant with Abram, saying, "To your descendants I give this land, from the river of Egypt to the great river, the river Euphrates."

Chapter 15: Claudia, Her Sisters, and the Ascension

John 17:20–26

"I ask not only on behalf of these, but also on behalf of those who will believe in me through their word, that they may all be one. As you, Father, are in me and I am in you, may they also be in us, so that the world may believe that you have sent me. The glory that you have given me I have given them, so that they may be one, as we are one, I in them and you in me, that they may become completely one, so that the world may know that you have sent me and have loved them even as you have loved me. Father, I desire that those also, whom you have given me, may be with me where I am, to see my glory, which you have given me because you loved me before the foundation of the world.

"Righteous Father, the world does not know you, but I know you; and these know that you have sent me. I made your name known to them, and I will make it known, so that the love with which you have loved me may be in them, and I in them."

Chapter 16: Lies and Secrets and Funerals

John 20:19–31

When it was evening on that day, the first day of the week, and the doors of the house where the disciples had met were locked for fear of the Jews, Jesus came and stood among them and said, "Peace be with you." After he said this, he showed them his hands and his side. Then the disciples rejoiced when they saw the Lord. Jesus said to them again, "Peace be with you. As the Father has sent me, so I send you." When he had said this, he breathed on them and said to them, "Receive the Holy Spirit. If you forgive the sins of any, they are forgiven them; if you retain the sins of any, they are retained."

But Thomas (who was called the Twin), one of the twelve, was not with them when Jesus came. So the other disciples told him, "We have seen the Lord." But he said to them, "Unless I see the mark of the nails in his hands, and put my finger in the mark of the nails and my hand in his side, I will not believe."

A week later his disciples were again in the house, and Thomas was with them. Although the doors were shut, Jesus came and stood among them and said, "Peace be with you." Then he said to Thomas, "Put your finger here and see my hands. Reach out your hand and put it in my side. Do not doubt but believe." Thomas answered him, "My Lord and my God!" Jesus said to him, "Have you believed because you have seen me? Blessed are those who have not seen and yet have come to believe."

Now Jesus did many other signs in the presence of his disciples, which are not written in this book. But these are written so that you may come to believe that Jesus is the Messiah, the Son of God, and that through believing you may have life in his name.

Chapter 17: Even This

Revelation 21:1–6

Then I saw a new heaven and a new earth; for the first heaven and the first earth had passed away, and the sea was no more. And I saw the holy city, the new Jerusalem, coming down out of heaven from God, prepared as a bride adorned for her husband. And I heard a loud voice from the throne saying,

> "See, the home of God is among mortals.
> He will dwell with them as their God;
> they will be his peoples,
> and God himself will be with them;
> he will wipe every tear from their eyes.
> Death will be no more;
> mourning and crying and pain will be no more,
> for the first things have passed away."

And the one who was seated on the throne said, "See, I am making all things new." Also he said, "Write this, for these words are trustworthy and true." Then he said to me, "It is done! I am the Alpha and the Omega, the beginning and the end. To the thirsty I will give water as a gift from the spring of the water of life."

Chapter 18: A Happier Place

Luke 4:21–30

Then he began to say to them, "Today this scripture has been fulfilled in your hearing." All spoke well of him and were amazed at the gracious words that came from his mouth. They said, "Is not this Joseph's son?" He said to them, "Doubtless you will quote to me this proverb, 'Doctor, cure yourself!' And you will say, 'Do here also in your hometown the things that we have heard you did at Capernaum.'" And he said, "Truly I tell you, no prophet is accepted in the prophet's hometown. But the truth is, there were many widows in Israel in the time of Elijah, when the heaven was shut up three years and six months, and there was a severe famine over all the land; yet Elijah was sent to none of them except to a widow at Zarephath in Sidon. There were also many lepers in Israel in the time of the prophet Elisha, and none of them was cleansed except Naaman the Syrian." When they heard this, all in the synagogue were filled with rage. They got up, drove him out of the town, and led him to the brow of the hill on which their town was built, so that they might hurl him off the cliff. But he passed through the midst of them and went on his way.

Chapter 19: Dirty Laundry

Hebrews 11:1–3, 8–16

Now faith is the assurance of things hoped for, the conviction of things not seen. Indeed, by faith our ancestors received approval. By faith we understand that the worlds were prepared by the word of God, so that what is seen was made from things that are not visible.

By faith Abraham obeyed when he was called to set out for a place that he was to receive as an inheritance; and he set out, not knowing where he was going. By faith he stayed for a time in the land he had been promised, as in a foreign land, living in the tents, as did Isaac and Jacob, who were heirs with him of the same promise. For he looked forward to the city that has foundations, whose architect and builder is God. By faith he received power of procreation, even though he was too old—and Sarah herself was barren—because he considered him faithful who had promised. Therefore from one person, and this one as good as dead, descendants were born, "as many as the stars of heaven and as the innumerable grains of sand by the seashore."

All of these died in faith without having received the promises, but from a distance they saw and greeted them. They confessed that they were strangers and foreigners on the earth, for people who speak in this way make it clear that they are seeking a homeland. If they had been thinking of the land that they had left behind, they would have had opportunity to return. But as it is, they desire a better country, that is, a heavenly one. Therefore God is not ashamed to be called their God; indeed, he has prepared a city for them.

Chapter 20: Until Morning

Luke 7:11–17

Soon afterwards he went to a town called Nain, and his disciples and a large crowd went with him. As he approached the gate of the town, a man who had died was being carried out. He was his mother's only son, and she was a widow; and with her was a large crowd from the town. When the Lord saw her, he had compassion for her and said to her, "Do not weep." Then he came forward and touched the bier, and the bearers stood still. And he said, "Young man, I say to you, rise!" The dead man sat up and began to speak, and Jesus gave him to his mother. Fear seized all of them; and they glorified God, saying, "A great prophet has risen among us!" and "God has looked favorably on his people!" This word about him spread throughout Judea and all the surrounding country.